On Keeping My Mouth Shut in Sunday School

PRAISE FOR *ON KEEPING MY MOUTH SHUT IN SUNDAY SCHOOL CLASS*

"In his brief, insightful, and highly recommended work, Jim Lutzweiler tells the stories of forgotten evangelical prophets of peace."

—William Kostlevy, Director,
Brethren Historical Library and Archives

"The congenial flow of Lutzweiler's unconventional Sunday school lesson contrasts effectively with his poignant questioning of church leaders and politicians who profess Christ but occasionally neglect his teachings about love, hate, and war. It is a fulsome challenge to insouciant conventional commentary."

—Ray Stevens, Professor of English Literature,
McDaniel University

"Lutzweiler provides an intimate look at contemporary Southern Baptist life in America. These sympathetic, insider reflections will help scholars better understand the dynamics of that faith community. It may enable readers to find parallels in other culturally and theologically conservative religious traditions attempting to negotiate both the larger culture and their internal idiocies. Astonishing to many will be the discussion of a Baptist pacifist (there is reportedly more than one). Equally interesting will be mentions of President Jimmy Carter, Dietrich Bonhoeffer, and a host of other iconic cultural figures. The author has provided a service by surprising us, offering the rare commodity of wisdom, and doing so in wonderfully enticing prose and poetry. The volume is an important contribution to the study of religion in the second decade of the twentieth century."

—David Bundy, Associate Director,
Manchester Wesley Research Centre,
Nazarene Theological College, Manchester, UK

"Jim Lutzweiler is every Sunday School teacher's nightmare—witty, probing, opinionated, unpredictable, skeptical, questioning, and above all challenging."

—JONATHAN ADDLETON, FORMER US AMBASSADOR TO MONGOLIA, AUTHOR OF *UNDERMINING THE CENTER*

"James Lutzweiler is not only a Sunday school teacher's nightmare but mine as well!"

—"SAINT" SHELLY LUTZWEILER, SPOUSE OF THE AUTHOR, A+ MOTHER

"I read this book not because I agree with everything in it, but because I enjoy Jim Lutzweiler's wit, sarcasm, and colorful descriptive language. In the process I have had some of my assumptions challenged. Pick it up and read a few pages and you will know what I mean."

—ERWIN LUTZER, PASTOR EMERITUS, THE MOODY CHURCH, CHICAGO

"As an outsider looking in, I marvel at the Christian fondness for padded crosses. Lutzweiler will make no friends reminding his fellow believers that Jesus was not hosting a potluck picnic but a prize fight with figurative plasma freely flowing."

—STEVE BAUGHMAN, AUTHOR OF *COVER-UP IN THE KINGDOM: PHONE SEX, LIES, AND GOD'S GREAT APOLOGIST, RAVI ZACHARIAS*

"My Bible student, James Lutzweiler, also used to pitch for the Pillsbury College Comets. He was a fine pitcher, primarily not because of his blazing fast ball that batters feared but because he was wild with it! I see from reading this that he is still fast and wild. We never won a lot of games but we had more fun than we were entitled to. And what he is pitching in this book will bring you more fun and facts than you might be entitled to. In this case the book, instead of a ballgame, is a winner. I laughed, cried, and occasionally screamed bloody murder!"

—CLARKE POORMAN, PROFESSOR OF BIBLE AND BASEBALL COACH, PILLSBURY BAPTIST BIBLE COLLEGE

"Jim Lutzweiler has neither won the Nobel Peace Prize nor occupied a chair of peace studies. This has not prevented him from thinking about peace and war or in speaking his thought. He offers here something you won't find in these sources, and they are thoughts that could come from no one else. They call for a hearing."

—WALLACE ALCORN, PASTOR, FIRST BAPTIST CHURCH, AUSTIN, MINNESOTA

"Lutzweiler writes like Max Lucado but with brass knuckles! I never had him for a Sunday school teacher but I did hear him preach a sermon once about Baptists, builders, and brothers. This book sounds to me more like one of his stem-winding sermons than a boring old lesson.

—LAWRENCE SCHRAM, BUSINESS PARTNER, BUILDER, AND CHRISTIAN BROTHER OF THE AUTHOR

"After reading this brief book, I feel a bit like I was playing against the Bears as I did forty years ago, catching short passes from Fran Tarkenton for critical first downs toward a touchdown. The book isn't long enough to be a 'Hail Mary' pass but it makes those kinds of low-percentage passes unnecessary with its biblical and progressive pitch for peacemaking. The Bears' Dick Butkus, All-Pro middle linebacker who dominated the field, also comes to mind in this connection. A play calling for a short pass over the middle brought about immediate terror to me. The imagery is not unlike the challenges we face daily, warring against principalities and powers that this hard-hitting author accentuates. Our opposition confronts us with fear and the intent to diminish our faith. Thanks be to God for his word, and for the fearless followers of Jesus like the peacemaking Apostle Paul and Tolstoy and Franz Jägerstätter and William Jennings Bryan, all of whom fought the good fight, finished the race, and kept the faith. My prayer is for others who come to read this book to experience the daily renewing of their minds so that their faith is readily present in all circumstances.

—DOUG KINGSRITER, FORMER MINNESOTA VIKINGS
TIGHT END AND WIDE RECEIVER

On Keeping My Mouth Shut in Sunday School

Being a Very Long Alternative Sunday School Lesson to the One I Just Heard

JAMES LUTZWEILER

foreword by William Kostlevy

RESOURCE *Publications* · Eugene, Oregon

ON KEEPING MY MOUTH SHUT IN SUNDAY SCHOOL
Being a Very Long Alternative Sunday School Lesson to the One I Just Heard

Resource Publications
An Imprint of Wipf and Stock Publishers
199 W. 8th Ave., Suite 3
Eugene, OR 97401

www.wipfandstock.com

PAPERBACK ISBN: 978-1-7252-7450-1
HARDCOVER ISBN: 978-1-7252-7451-8
EBOOK ISBN: 978-1-7252-7452-5

Manufactured in the U.S.A.   06/09/20

Dedicated[1] to the memory of some mostly lesser-known
Sunday school teachers, Past and Present:

Simeon Jocelyn

John D. Rockefeller

James Garfield

Stonewall Jackson

Sam Houston[2]

Jesse James[3]

Dwight L. Moody

John Wanamaker

Charlie Soong

Alvin York

Rosalie Willson[4]

1. So far as I know, this is the first-ever footnoted dedication page in American publishing history. Names appear in approximate chronological order. Key word: "approximate."

2. This is admittedly a tendentious claim. I have no hard evidence that Sam ever taught Sunday school. I only know that eventually every Southern Baptist teaches a class sometime in his life, even one I know of who eventually became an agnostic but continued teaching. True story. If I am wrong about Sam, I will repudiate this claim at the Last Judgment along with a lot of other things too noxious to note here.

3. Some biographer of Jesse James has alleged this. We know his father was a Southern Baptist.

4. Rosalie Willson was the mother and Sunday school teacher of Meredith Willson(MW). Among other songs, MW wrote *76 Trombones* for the musical, *The Music Man, May the Good Lord Bless and Keep You, Till There Was You,* and *It's Beginning to Look a Lot Like Christmas.* In MW's autobiography entitled *And There I stood with My Piccolo,* he relates a story about what happened one day in his Sunday school class. I repeated his story in Sunday school one Sunday and the teacher and half the class (average age 125 years —or more) all of whom had urology problems of some sort thought I was uncouth. Readers can decide. The story appears in Exhibit H way way ahead.

Elizabeth Sanford[5]
Elmer Towns
Mrs. Wally Amos Criswell[6]
Willie Nelson
The Red Bishop[7]
David Smiley[8]
Ken Starr
Jimmy Carter
Zig Ziglar
Vernon Lyons[9]
"Saint" Shelly Lutzweiler[10]

5. Elizabeth Sanford was the Sunday school teacher of Terry Sanford. Sanford later became the Governor of North Carolina, JFK's pick to replace J. Edgar Hoover, a U.S. Senator, and the president of Duke University. Loved by everyone, he got in trouble with his old Sunday school teacher, when the press reported that Governor Sanford was serving wine at social functions in the governor's Mansion. His teacher was also his mother.

6. The spouse of Billy Graham's pastor, Wally Amos Criswell.

7. Hint: His initials are P.P. and he served as president of the Southern Baptist Convention sometime circa 1998. He is a great white hunter whose nickname is "Dr. Death," and he is the Bill Gothard-ish honorary grandpa of the author. He created a commentary on the Book of *Revelation* that is in Jimmy Carter's personal library. He once had red hair. It is now gray and very thin.

8. The late David Smiley taught American history for half a century at Wake Forest University. He taught a Sunday school class that was broadcast over the radio from a studio in Winston-Salem. Until it disappeared, there was a beautiful tribute to Smiley online. It can still be had by requesting a copy from the author who has preserved it. It features a never-before-published picture of Jane Mansfield and Smiley.

9. Vernon Lyons is the long time pastor (seventy years so far) of the Ashburn Baptist Church in the Chicago suburb of Orland Park. He was the inspiration for Rev. Vernon in the *Left Behind* series by Jerry Jenkins and Tim LaHaye.

10. See review by "Saint" Shelly Lutzweiler elsewhere in this book. Placed last on this list because the last shall be first.

Contents

Foreword

"If WW I was the Kingdom of God, maybe we need to give hell a chance." So writes James Lutzweiler in response to an enthusiastic letter of a war supporter to President Woodrow Wilson. The sentence captures the spirit of this thought provoking, ironic, irreverent, and illuminating study of the misplaced patriotism in American Christianity, especially in its Evangelical and Baptist expressions. But to be honest, one could write separate volumes on similar Methodist, Holiness, Episcopal, Catholic, Orthodox, and even Pentecostal compromises with Moloch.

As appropriate for a book entitled *On Keeping My Mouth Shut in Sunday School*, it begins with an opening prayer by that famous of Civil War Confederate draft dodgers, Mark Twain. It follows with the actual Sunday school lesson, an account of how a famous Christian pacifist, Alvin York became a Hollywood fabricated war hero in spite of his growing reservation about the First World War itself. This is followed by the real heart of the book: nine exhibits of famous and not so-famous Christians struggling with war and its implications for followers of Jesus.

As an actual conscientious objector of war (I have the draft card to prove it), my own views differ slightly from Lutzweiler's. His is the chastened view that war maybe be necessary but is always tragic and involves deep loss and suffering. Evangelicals and Baptists will learn four important lessons from this valuable Sunday school lesson. First, in the spirit of Barbara Tuchman's *March of Folly* and Edmund Wilson's *Patriotic Gore*, war, especially WWI, was a tragedy that led inevitably to a second tragic global slaughter.

Secondly, there are forgotten heroes such as the Southern Baptist pastor, J. J. Taylor, who could not be stampeded into war. Thirdly, the nuanced studies of Alvin York and Dietrich Bonhoeffer remind us of the complexity of the issues at hand and the challenges of following the Prince of Peace in a world where clear cut answers to complex questions are not always available. Finally, Lutzweiler is especially adept at the subtle specifics always present in the historical record including stories of the son of a Baptist missionary leading FDR into a justifiable war, or Billy Graham gaining access to the inner sanctuary of presidential power by justifying military actions or William Jennings Bryan warning Woodrow Wilson that US involvement in WW I on the side of Britain and France that was setting the stage for an even greater war. This is a gripping and important book for all Christians regardless of denominational label.

Dr. William Kostlevy
Director Brethren Historical Library and Archives
March 2020

Preface

At present (March 2020), I have no idea what the title of this book will be. The title I have chosen and used when I sent it out to friends and enemies for review is *On Keeping My Mouth Shut in Sunday School Class: Being a Very Long Alternative Sunday School Lesson to the One I Just Heard.* It's the identical title I sent to the publisher who accepted it on that basis. However, that title is a mouthful and not altogether euphonic. It's chief merit is that that is exactly what this book is: a Sunday school lesson, as I would teach it to my fellow Southern Baptists and to anybody else for that matter, pagan or pilgrim in progress. And I wrote it up immediately after hearing the lesson to which I refer in it upon which proclamation I nearly puked.

The reason I have no idea if my chosen title will stick is because I have no control over it. The publisher does, and the publisher has to sell copies in order for both of us not to go under any further. There are other titles that are just as good though they might be a bit cryptic at first glance. I suggest, for example, *A Sunday School Lesson for Every Last Southern Baptist* or even *Poop on Easter* (Yes, I know, I know, that sounds wild, but just stay tuned for a few more paragraphs. It will make sense. Sad sense) or *An Apology to the Ghost of Dietrich Bonhoeffer.* Something like these latter words actually appears in Exhibit G, an exhibit I added after sending everything else up to that point out for reviewers. I like feedback to my meditations and routinely plague friends and foes alike for their reflections and my tuition-free continuing education. More often than not, they ignore them, as there are far too many for them to read. I never leave a thought unpublished and uncirculated.

However, in the case of this alternate Sunday school lesson, minus Exhibit G, a former U.S. Ambassador who believed somewhat like I did about Dietrich Bonhoeffer nevertheless asked me what my evidence was for Bonhoeffer's complicity in the assassination attempts on Hitler. This is a topic I address in Exhibits A, B, and C. After thinking about his question and researching it, I have added Exhibit G in order to fine tune my view. In this case "fine tune" is a euphemism for "repudiate to some degree." Exhibit G should be self-explanatory and even paradigmatic for those who have no idea how to apologize. Their tribe is vast and I have no problem being in the vanguard.

Exhibit G should also be an illustration of what should go on in a Sunday school class: frank and robust exchanges such as I had with the Ambassador. Often it does not, and I am just as much to blame as the next Sunday school scholar. I do not like to stir up a hornet's nest. I like to be liked. What I like most about Sunday school is Sunday school picnics, fond remembrances of which now stretch back for maybe seventy years for me. This Sunday school lesson is an exception to the rule. Above all I intend it to be a service to anyone who reads it, exponential profits being only an incredibly close second.

I would add one more service in the process. Having apologized to Bonhoeffer's ghost, I do not apologize for the following. I have long suspected, admittedly tendentiously, that Bonhoeffer has been a heretic in dimensions not just political but theological. My own theology professor in seminary lumped the Lutheran literary laureate in with the God-Is-Dead theologians [sic?] like Thomas J.J. Altizer, et al. I tried reading Bonhoeffer but gave up, finding this Nazi prisoner's prose more abstruse than a combination of my own and that of James Joyce, Karl Barth, and a Mexican drug dealer and user thrown in for lagniappe. Accordingly, I have sent more than one memo to my dear friend and occasionally irascible but world-class theological bibliographer, John Warwick Montgomery, asking him what Bonhoeffer really believed. Suspecting me, probably correctly, of being lazy for asking him to do my homework, he semi-graciously put me off with simple generalities that he just didn't like Bonhoeffer's theology —without telling me what it was he didn't like.

Finally, no doubt frustrated with my biblical importunity and not long after the Ides of March 2020, the prolific and prickly professor sent me an essay by Richard Weikart that answered every essential question I ever had about Bonhoeffer's theology. In brief, Weikart, who gives every evidence of having done his homework that I would not want to do, tells us that Bonhoeffer considered the historical bodily resurrection of Jesus to be a myth. I trust Weikart's scholarship. The net effect of this assessment is that the entire collected works of Bonhoeffer can in my view be reduced to three simple and very sad words: "Poop on Easter." This, too, is a euphemism. Had Bonhoeffer referred to the Holocaust as a "myth," he would have been hanged by Zionists and Evangelicals alike instead of by the Nazis. Yet his view has filtered down from many similar streams into Southern Baptist seminaries like its flagship in Louisville, where one professor, Eric Rust, for years and still in his surviving books taught students that not only the resurrection but the virgin birth and other cardinal evangelical doctrines are myths.

Readers of these words about just Bonhoeffer, not Rust, can check up on these claims by reading for themselves Weikart's essay entitled "Scripture and Myth in Dietrich Bonhoeffer."[11] Thanks to Bill Gates, about whose views on the resurrection I have no earthly idea, they can read Weikart's essay online.[12] This citation alone is worth whatever you paid for this book even if it was the $100.00 or more that it is really worth. Those who appreciate it can send a thank you note to Dr. Weikart with perhaps a token love offering for writing it and its coming to my attention and now to yours and to whomever you might gift it. Just tell them Bonhoeffer is a killer-carrier of ecclesiastical coronavirus and let that short sentence be your own book.

I have asked my good friend Bill Kostlevy to write a Foreword for this collage of meditations and exhibits. I have no idea what he will write. I tell anyone I ask for such a favor to write anything they want, complimentary or defamatory. If, of course, Bill writes anything defamatory, I will sue the publisher for all I am worth. This

11. *Fides et Historia* 25,1 (1993): 12—25.

12. https://www.csustan.edu/sites/default/files/History/Faculty/Weikart/Scripture-and-Myth-in-Dietrich-Bonhoeffer.pdf.

should cause no fears. In spite of any appearances, I have written nothing defamatory myself, though if I had a middle name, as my Sunday-school-teaching sister has said, it would be "Volcano," as in "Vesuvius," for a mere fraction of the literary lava I have spewed all over the place. Jesus said he prefers his followers to be hot or cold. No one I know has ever called James V. O'Lutzweiler lukewarm.

There are probably more than two reasons for keeping my mouth shut anymore in Sunday school but I can only think of two right now. The first occurred one Sunday morning not long ago, when the lesson was about Moses and the Israelites crossing the Red Sea. The teacher asked for anyone to comment. I did. I brought up a story about the crossing of the Red Sea that songwriter Meredith Willson tells about in his delightful memoir entitled *And There I Stood with My Piccolo*. That story appears in Exhibit H, way ahead of here, which I added after I thought I was all through writing this book. In short, my dear reader, if you are ever at a party where attendees are all competing to produce the best story of the evening, whip out this swashbuckling tale by Willson and shamelessly crush your wannabe superiors with this biblical jewel. It is why I included Willson's otherwise obscure mother on the Dedication page of this tutorial.

The second reason involves the best-selling *Left Behind* series by Tim LaHaye and Jerry Jenkins and their theological predecessor and one-time prisoner, Cyrus Ingerson Scofield, of *Scofield Reference Bible* fame. I forget what the overall lesson was about; however in it the Mormons came up as a topic. The teacher explained how the Mormons, none of which were present, "added" to the Scriptures. I couldn't and wouldn't challenge that, nor do I think any self-respecting Mormon would. But I don't worry about Mormons. I worry about what we Evangelicals add to the Scriptures. I proceeded to refer to the "baloney" Scofield and his theological descendants like LaHaye and Jenkins added to the Scriptures. Just one tiny word: "Baloney!" However, most in the classroom were such descendants of Scofield and there were maybe another thousand or so in their own classes within a football field's length of where I sat, when I erupted as if I were Popocatepetl. The class then went as silent as I now intend to be myself from here on out, but I heard about it later. Not much later. In the car going home. You get my drift. And then later by email from the teacher who told me about complaints he had received from those who are directed by the Bible to approach those with whom they differ one-on-one. You would think Mount St. Helens had erupted again, all over some simple baloney instead of tectonic plates shifting or doing whatever tectonic plates do, while we are sleeping.

In an email exchange shortly after that class, the teacher of it informed me that because of my challenge, he had re-examined the subject one afternoon and had come away still believing in the pre-tribulation rapture of the church. I envied his ability to learn so fast without consulting any of the sources to the contrary. I know my dear friend, Dr. E. Michael Rusten, had spent a thousand hours or two writing for New York University his PhD dissertation entitled "A Critical Evaluation of Dispensational Interpretations of the Book of Revelation," and I doubted if said teacher had ever read it or even knew it existed, to say nothing of Ernest Sandeen's magisterial meditations in his book entitled *The Roots of Fundamentalism* or the many treatments of this fantasy of the future by Dave MacPherson or my own incredible essay about Scofield, a painfully short abstract of which I have attached as a final Exhibit, Exhibit I. Those interested in more of that historically informative piece might wish to chip in for its inclusion in the Second Edition of this book. Whatever the case, the irony is that my "Baloney" ended up confirming the teacher in a view that millions of wiser Bible students have now left far behind. Then I prayed the sinner's prayer: "God be merciful to me, an idiotic scholar who never should have called out, 'Baloney!' I repent! And this book will be my public confession."

And now, with no further adieu, let us open the rest of this class with prayer. I call upon the late Mark Twain to offer it.

JAMES LUTZWEILER
Archivist (1999–2013), Southeastern Baptist Theological Seminary
Schnappsburg Poet Laureate (1982—present)
Concert pianist trapped in an aging amateur's body (2020—?)
Easter Sunday 2020

An Opening Prayer by Mark Twain

It was a time of great and exalting excitement. The country was up in arms, the war was on, in every breast burned the holy fire of patriotism; the drums were beating, the bands playing, the toy pistols popping, the bunched firecrackers hissing and spluttering; on every hand and far down the receding and fading spread of roofs and balconies a fluttering wilderness of flags flashed in the sun; daily the young volunteers marched down the wide avenue gay and fine in their new uniforms, the proud fathers and mothers and sisters and sweethearts cheering them with voices choked with happy emotion as they swung by; nightly the packed mass meetings listened, panting, to patriot oratory with stirred the deepest deeps of their hearts, and which they interrupted at briefest intervals with cyclones of applause, the tears running down their cheeks the while; in the churches the pastors preached devotion to flag and country, and invoked the God of Battles beseeching His aid in our good cause in outpourings of fervid eloquence which moved every listener.

It was indeed a glad and gracious time, and the half dozen rash spirits that ventured to disapprove of the war and cast a doubt upon its righteousness straightway got such a stern and angry warning that for their personal safety's sake they quickly shrank out of sight and offended no more in that way.

Sunday morning came—next day the battalions would leave for the front; the church was filled; the volunteers were there, their young faces alight with martial dreams—visions of the stern advance, the gathering momentum, the rushing charge, the flashing sabers, the flight of the foe, the tumult, the enveloping smoke, the fierce pursuit, the surrender!

Then home from the war, bronzed heroes, welcomed, adored, submerged in golden seas of glory! With the volunteers sat their dear ones, proud, happy, and envied by the neighbors and friends who had no sons and brothers to send forth to the field of honor, there to win for the flag, or, failing, die the noblest of noble deaths. The service proceeded; a war chapter from the Old Testament was read; the first prayer was said; it was followed by an organ burst that shook the building, and with one impulse the house rose, with glowing eyes and beating hearts, and poured out that tremendous invocation:

> *God the all-terrible! Thou who ordainest,*
> *Thunder thy clarion and lightning thy sword!*

Then came the "long" prayer. None could remember the like of it for passionate pleading and moving and beautiful language. The burden of its supplication was, that an ever-merciful and benignant Father of us all would watch over our noble young soldiers, and aid, comfort, and encourage them in their patriotic work; bless them, shield them in the day of battle and the hour of peril, bear them in His mighty hand, make them strong and confident, invincible in the bloody onset; help them crush the foe, grant to them and to their flag and country imperishable honor and glory.

An aged stranger entered and moved with slow and noiseless step up the main aisle, his eyes fixed upon the minister, his long body clothed in a robe that reached to his feet, his head bare, his white hair descending in a frothy cataract to his shoulders, his seamy face unnaturally pale, pale even to ghastliness. With all eyes following him and wondering, he made his silent way; without pausing, he ascended to the preacher's side and stood there waiting. With shut lids the preacher, unconscious of his presence, continued his moving prayer, and at last finished it with the words, uttered in fervent appeal, "Bless our arms, grant us the victory, O Lord and God, Father and Protector of our land and flag!"

The stranger touched his arm, motioned him to step aside—which the startled minister did—and took his place. During some moments he surveyed the spellbound audience with solemn eyes, in which burned an uncanny light; then in a deep voice he said: "I come from the Throne—bearing a message from Almighty God!" The words smote the house with a shock; if the stranger perceived it he gave no attention. "He has heard the prayer of His servant your shepherd, and will grant it if such be your desire after I, His messenger, shall have explained to you its import—that is to say, its full import. For it is like unto many of the prayers of men, in that it asks for more than he who utters it is aware of—except he pause and think. "God's servant and yours has prayed his prayer. Has he paused and taken thought? Is it one prayer? No, it is two—one uttered, and the other not. Both have reached the ear of Him who heareth all supplications, the spoken and the unspoken. Ponder this—keep it in mind. If you would beseech a blessing upon yourself, beware! lest without intent you invoke a curse upon your neighbor at the same time. If you pray for the blessing of rain on your crop which needs it, by that act you are possibly praying for a curse on some neighbor's crop which may not need rain and can be injured by it.

"You have heard your servant's prayer—the uttered part of it. I am commissioned by God to put into words the other part of it—that part which the pastor—and also you in your hearts—fervently prayed silently. And ignorantly and unthinkingly? God grant that it was so! You heard the words 'Grant us the victory, O Lord our God!' That is sufficient. The whole of the uttered prayer is compact into those pregnant words. Elaborations were not necessary. When you have prayed for victory you have prayed for many unmentioned results which follow victory—must follow it, cannot help but follow it. Upon the listening spirit of God fell also the unspoken part of the prayer. He commandeth me to put it into words. Listen!

> "Lord our Father, our young patriots, idols of our hearts, go forth into battle—be Thou near them! With them—in spirit—we also go forth from the sweet peace of our beloved firesides to smite the foe. O Lord our God, help us tear their soldiers to bloody shreds with our shells; help us to cover their smiling fields with the pale forms of their patriot dead; help us to drown the thunder of the guns with the shrieks of their wounded, writhing in pain; help us to lay waste their humble homes with

a hurricane of fire; help us to wring the hearts of their unoffending widows with unavailing grief; help us to turn them out roofless with their little children to wander unfriended in the wastes of their desolated land in rags and hunger and thirst, sports of the sun flames in summer and the icy winds of winter, broken in spirit, worn with travail, imploring thee for the refuge of the grave and denied it.

For our sakes who adore Thee, Lord, blast their hopes, blight their lives, protract their bitter pilgrimmage, make heavy their steps, water their way with their tears, stain the white snow with the blood of their wounded feet!"[13]

13. https://warprayer.org/

The Actual Lesson

Gradually I am learning to keep my big mouth shut. Even in Sunday school. I say too many things to people that are radical and that shake them up. I blame Jesus for that, of course, as "turning the other cheek" is just one of the numerous crazy, disgusting, and effeminate things he told his followers to do. Same with the dirtball North Carolina Governor, James Martin, who once quoted that milquetoast and pansy poet, John Greenleaf Whittier, as having said, "Peace makes greater demands upon manhood than war."[1] What? Peacemakers have bigger cajones than Patton? What is this world coming to?

In all events I would rather open my mouth in obscure essays and period pieces like this one that no one is ever likely to read and get upset over. As the Commie Vladimir Lenin once surprisingly said, quoting a poem by the tutor of the Czar's children and the Christian poet, Zhukovsky, slightly paraphrased but close to verbatim, "We all have crosses to bear and we are constantly trying on different ones for a good fit."[2] As for me, I like my crosses padded and painless, pointedly even pleasurable. There! I just did it again!

What prompts this soon-to-be-forgotten meditation is a Sunday school class from which just moments ago I narrowly escaped with my resolve to shut up almost totally intact. The Sunday school class in question was about murder. The text was Deuteronomy 5:17

1. The quote from Governor Martin appeared in a now long lost speech he delivered one year at a celebration in Whittier, North Carolina, a town named after one of the poet's relatives. A copy is in my possession.

2. Payne, p. 209.

that proscribes murder as one of the fruits of the spirit. I had a lot I could have said about the subject, especially in view of the fact that I once gave serious consideration to killing a shyster lawyer who ran off with over $1,000,000 of my real estate and got away with the theft. Long story for elsewhere. But I had a lot more besides that to say about murder, none of which I did. Until now.

Before the teacher got into the lesson, he asked for prayer requests. There were many, mostly for family and friends suffering from various ills. I suffer from numerous ills myself, but I have always found that a big plate of Texas brisket washed down with inordinate doses of frozen potato juice is good for all the things that ail me from common colds to erectile dysfunction (for the relief of which I have never yet heard a Sunday school supplicant request prayer). The teacher, Bob Cooke, makes some of the finest brisket I have ever eaten or expect to eat; and his serving of it for a Sunday school social a few weeks earlier is what initially suckered me into this mostly moribund class in which I wished to cause absolutely no commotion.

In addition to the text Bob grilled on the blackboard, as if it were Biblical brisket, and juxtaposed to the warning words "Do not murder," there was a list of acts that incorporated what Bob had in mind by murder: homicide, abortion, euthanasia, suicide, assisted suicide, and opioids. I don't much believe in abortion, of course, especially late-term and even post-18 variety, when the still-little pups are sent off to war. In fact, glaringly missing from the grocery list of murderous methods was "war," as if that national pastime had not yet risen to the level of murder. By definition, of course, Navy Seal Edward Gallagher in the service of capital punishment never even laid a glove on that young wounded ISIS fighter. It was technically the knife in Gallagher's hand that did the dirty work; and that inanimate metal must be the one to give an account to God for murder at the Last Judgment. Missing, too, were "words." Words can kill, too, though they can also give life. But that theme must wait for another day.

I had actually been thinking about murder and war just before arriving at class because of the sermon I had heard minutes earlier. I think about that subject a lot in my life, having luckily survived the

Vietnam War without a scratch or a single firefight. Truth be told, I had a college deferment so I missed it all; however, while putting myself through graduate school, I used to work for a funeral home. There I witnessed the flag-draped corpses of my contemporaries in their coffins. In all events in that Sunday morning's routinely boring sermon by the young pup who prattles them, he made reference to Leo Tolstoy. Tolstoy never ceases to remind me of war, not only that of 1812 but such wars as Vietnam and the shameful peace that eventually followed. Technically, the preacher's reference was first of all to Tennessee Williams but then quickly thereafter to a short story entitled *Something from Tolstoy* that Williams had written back in 1931.

The preacher in question began to review Tennessee's entire story, in the process plagiarizing his charming narrative word-for-word from a summary of it already on the internet. In point of fact it would appear that he plagiarized it from a site, Bible.org, that in turn had plagiarized it from another site![3] But I did not realize this until going home and Googling it and finding it on several sites. At the time I heard the plagiarizer tell it, I was thinking to myself, "This lad is far more literate than I realized," and I was embarrassed at my own ill literacy. But now I know better. In all events he then told us how we as a congregation were just like one of the characters in Tennessee's Tolstoyan story. But never once did he tell us exactly or even remotely how we were "just" like him. His was all the thrill of the chase but none of the danger. This has occurred many times. It will happen again.

3. While I cannot be certain because the young pup never replies to his emails, it would appear that he got his Tennessee Williams story from a website at https://bible.org/illustration/forgotten-love. This site in turn appears to have downloaded the story from another website at http://www.adathisraelshul. org/e-torah/parsha/30-behar-bchukotai/623-let-s-table-the-discussion-behar-bechukosai-5775. God alone knows if that website got it from another website. I don't have the time to chase this rabbit. But one thing is clear. The pup in question was not the original creator of the verbatim narrative he spun for us. And, ironically, there can be no doubt that some of the folks who left that service thought it was a great sermon, conflating the pup's plagiarized material with the remaining thirty minutes of the boring sermon itself! Superstitious 19th century Russian peasants had nothing on this thoughtless group in 20th century High Point, North Carolina.

Tennessee's tale was one of my only two takeaways from the service. The second was a determination to read the complete story by Williams. The first takeaway was Tolstoy himself. While I have never read his famous *War and Peace* (I once heard Woody Allen say he read it once after taking a speed-reading course, quipping afterwards, "I think the book is about Russia"), I have read Tolstoy's far lesser-known but mind-blowing book *The Kingdom of God is Within You*. My own copy of that stem-winder was published in 1925 by The Kremlin Press about which Press I know nothing, and I have often wondered if it was located in Moscow and run by Uncle Joe's Commies. After all, Stalin himself was a reader and admirer of Tolstoy and Dostoyevsky, both Christian writers. Why wouldn't a Bolshevik publish Tolstoy's books?

In all events, Tolstoy's *Kingdom of God* book is for the most part a commentary on the Sermon on the Mount that was preached by the Master of ministers. In it, Tolstoy expounds upon the case against murder and war, a case absorbed by the likes of Gandhi, Martin Luther King, Jr., and others. I will not attempt to review the book here except to say that no one can mention Tolstoy's name to me without my thinking of this provocative book and murder and war. The young minister in question mentioned Tolstoy only in passing. But that is all it took for me to be psyched up about war, as I entered the classroom devoted to murder and its proscription.

I had already determined prior to class that I would say nothing in class or at least as little as I possibly could. Re-read my Preface, if necessary. This was in deference to my poor wife who goes into cardiac arrest practically every time I speak in such venues. For me the most exciting thing in life is whatever I plan to say next. For her it is pure torture. So I bolted my lips tighter than a nun's chastity belt and percolated pyrotechnically in private over what I would say, in case the damns dammed back by my tightly-clenched dentures should burst forth.

I succeeded totally except for two tiny leaks. When Bob suddenly raised the recent subject of the assassination of Qassem Soleimani, I involuntarily blurted out, "You're not going to open that can of worms, are you, Bob?"[4] And later when the discussion came up

4.. Here I could have opened several cans of worms myself, beginning with the actual assassin, Herschel Grynszpan, and continuing through the wannabe assassin, Dietrich Bonhoefer. Few people have ever heard the name of Herschel Grynszpan, but most literate people have heard of Kristallnacht, the Night of the Broken Glass, in Germany on November 9–10, 1938. Both can easily be Googled. For many years I sort of uncritically thought that Kristallnacht just happened out of the blue. When it dawned on me that that did not make any sense, I discovered Herschel Grynszpan who on November 7, 1938, assassinated a German embassy official in Paris. Though it is true that the German response involved a bit of overkill, sometimes that is what happens after assassinations. In fact, far more people were killed as a result of the assassination of Qassem Soleimani on January 3, 2020, than were killed by the Germans on November 9–10, 1938. And, amazingly enough, when Grynszpan fell into the hands of the Germans, the Germans never killed him even though he was a Jew. In this connection one is reminded of Sam Houston after the Battle of San Jacinto. Every red-blooded Texan was calling for the scalp of Santa Anna for his murderous conduct at the Alamo, but Sam Houston (who was not even saved by the Southern Baptists until maybe twenty years later) would not yield to their importunities, and he sent the unlucky "Napoleon of the West" back to Mexico. And what was the result? Santa Anna lived long enough to lose Arizona, New Mexico, Utah, Nevada, Colorado, and California as well, which we must admit was not a bad return on Sam's exercise of restraint. Then, of course, there is the case of wannabe assassin Rev. Bonhoeffer who joined in with those who thought it would be a good idea to assassinate Hitler. I wrote a sketch of Bonhoeffer for a book entitled *Churchfails*, published by Broadman and Holman. *Churchfails* is a compilation of sketches of 100 individuals from church history who have made serious blunders. I contributed eighteen of those sketches, but my contribution on Bonhoeffer was censored out by the editors. The unstated reason was because I posed the question, "Whom would Jesus assassinate?" The publisher had a nice market for Bonhoeffer's writings and did not want that status quo disturbed by such an interrogatory. So out the window went my questioning of the validity of assassination as a fruit of the spirit. Accordingly, I am attaching that rejected sketch hereto as Appendix B. I might add that one of the associate pastors of the Green Street Baptist Church also rejected the sketch. In an ostensible sermon one Sunday morning the Rev. Quentin Self lauded Bonhoeffer as a "martyr," a characterization to which I felt the Lord pressuring me to challenge this even younger pup than his pastor. So I did in a letter, a letter which appears hereinafter as Appendix C. Br'er Self has yet to reply to it, thereby exhibiting something I do not wish to characterize in a family essay like this. All of which is to say that if the law of unintended consequences means anything at all, I'm not so sure assassination is the solution it is cracked up to be. I have even argued in other venues that if France had only invested $9 billion in its wonderful pastries for the Germans after WWI instead of constructing the utterly worthless Maginot Line

about guns in church, I asked for a raise of hands of those in class who might be carrying any of them. No hands went up, though Bob indicated that there were those in the congregation who did carry them. And with those two minor infractions, neither of which addressed my observations on war, I lasted until the last prayer was uttered and the class dismissed. I deserve an A+.

What I should have said and would have said, if I were not a chicken and did not like my crosses padded, would have been about World War I as a case in point. WWII and Vietnam are still too current in order to have a reasonable conversation about them. Practically no one knows anything about WWI and I thought I might be on safe ground to call into question the legitimacy of that exercise in wanton murder. Whether I would have been safe or not is moot, as I did not raise the subject. But if I had, the following is what I would have said.

First of all, I would have raised the subject pleasantly, at least as pleasantly as one can raise the subject of this Molocaust (a "Molocaust" is a holocaust raised to a couple of exponential powers, and it derives from the Old Testament god, Moloch, to whom human sacrifices, often live babies, were made). I had just seen the brand new movie 1917 a few days earlier and could easily have launched into my own verbal bombs and gospel gas with reference to it. Suffice it to say that the movie was a bloody and totally unrealistic affair and had nothing to do with the morality of its occurrence. But it's good for an oblique entry into this topic.

For the purposes of the rest of these meditations, let us assume that WWI was totally wrong, at least from the standpoint of America's involvement in it. I would argue the same moral criminality for all of Europe as well, but Europe is not my sphere here. Just America and just High Point, North Carolina, for the moment. I call as my first witness one of the most celebrated and decorated

---

for the same expenditure that maybe WWII might have been avoided or at least scaled way back. Ah, but I hallucinate. But at least I do not hallucinate alone. So did an unidentified American newspaper reporter in the period 1914–1918 who wrote for consumers, Christian and non-Christian alike, that the Germans were crucifying babies —the very kind of atrocity story that Christians with presumably transformed minds lap up like a puppy in his milk dish.

American soldiers in that debacle: Alvin York. I tell the full story of Alvin York in an essay I wrote some time back. I am attaching it hereafter as an Exhibit, Exhibit A to be exact. That Exhibit is one reason this written Sunday school class is over 100 pages long (at present). But in brief, here is the short story of Alvin York, as if Tennessee Williams or Leo Tolstoy or even O. Henry or O'Lutzweiler from Greensboro might have told it.

Alvin York was a hell-raiser in his youth near Jamestown, Tennessee (Ironically, I write at this moment in Jamestown, North Carolina, near High Point). After a conversion experience, York joined the church there of a small sect that had formed during the Civil War as a result of its opposition to war in general and that one —erroneously called "irrepressible"— in particular. He began teaching a Sunday school class in that church and came across the commandment not to kill —the exact same commandment under consideration on the blackboard in our Sunday school class at Green Street Baptist Church in High Point, North Carolina, on Sunday morning, January 19, 2020 at 9:45 a.m. York concluded that killing was wrong and he taught that to the young people under his tutelage. Then America became involved in WWI and the U.S. Army got hold of York.

Though recently converted to Christ and peacemaking, York was born again again by the U.S. Army, and off he went to France. There in an amazing episode about which you can read in my essay or online by Googling him, York became a decorated hero and the subject of parades and emoluments upon his return to America. But as the years went by after WWI, York became disillusioned and concluded that the war did not really accomplish what Woodrow Wilson had suggested it would do: to make the world safe for democracy and be the war to end all wars. By the eve of WWII, which anyone with brains will tell you was caused by WWI, York had reverted toward the pacifism of his youth and church.

Then Hollywood got hold of the WWI hero. Those who had an interest in getting America involved in WWII approached York about making a movie of his life and his killing of several Germans that he likened to a simple turkey shoot back home in Tennessee. The movie moguls beat Jesus to death again, and once again York succumbed to the Sirenic and Molochan calls for human sacrifice that WWI had brought about partly by his own participation in it. The movie had spectacular results, causing men to enlist like few other stimulants did; and it made Americans loathe their old hero, Charles Lindbergh, who opposed America's entry into WWII for some very good reasons. Leaving aside for now the morality of America's entry into WWII, it is interesting to note in light of Green Street Baptist Church's affiliation with the Southern Baptist Convention, it was the son of Southern Baptist missionaries to Japan who in the days prior to December 7, 1941, wrote a memo for the Pentagon and President Roosevelt about how to provoke the Japanese into firing the first shot that would bring us into the conflict.[5] Surprise!

I had never before heard of Alvin York or the movie about his life until driving one day to Nashville, Tennessee, and passing on I-40 an exit sign that pointed to the Alvin York Memorial to the North. I never pulled off to explore it but wondered who he was. I have lived most of my life under a rock. The first time I heard of him in any detail was at a Wednesday night church supper at the Dillon Road Baptist Church in Jamestown, North Carolina, where one of York's distant cousins attended. Then I watched the movie. Then I read up on him on the internet. Then I made the pilgrimage to Jamestown, Tennessee, to visit the Memorial to him and the crumbling remains of a Bible college the old soldier had attempted but failed to create. After all these stimuli, it was an easy segue to see the utter insanity of WWI and those naive American boys who like York went off to the killing fields of France. In a word, WWI was simply wrong. End of story.

Remote as it was from my own birthday in 1946, I was still a loser because of WWI even though I never fought in it. My uncle Bill did. He was mustard-gassed in France; and when he returned

---

5. See the startling book *Day of Deceit: The Truth about FDR and Pearl Harbor* (Free Press, 1999) by Robert Stinnett. See https://en.wikipedia.org/wiki/Day_of_Deceit. The name of the son of the missionaries is Arthur McCollum. You can read about him at the following url in case Stinnett's book is not in your library: https://en.wikipedia.org/wiki/Arthur_H._McCollum. See also my sermon entitled "Lesser Known Baptists" reproduced in Appendix D hereinafter.

to Philadelphia, where I was born, he majored in fermented fluids rather than Philly cheese steaks in order to blot out the horrors he had seen overseas. When he died, he left me $50 with which I bought a brand new Schwinn bicycle. Had Uncle Bill gone into the oil business instead of into war, as did J. Paul Getty, he might have left me $500,000 to buy a Rolls Royce instead of that shiny new bike. WWI simply cost me a bundle, too.

What has come to amuse me now that I have come to understand it is how American evangelicals have largely sided with murderous hawks, when it comes to war, but have vigorously opposed the visitation of soldiers with prostitutes, when it comes to the same subject. They are willing to overlook murder by euphemizing it down to "State" killing but show no interest in overlooking "State" fornication. A classic example of one having this myopic mindset is none other than Woodrow Wilson, even though he was never a typical evangelical.

Hypocrite Woodrow himself engaged in fornication, though apparently not of the State variety, if the story of the president and Mrs. Peck whom he pecked has any validity; and I think it does. But then so did MLK, Gandhi, and, sad to say, Tolstoy himself. But when it came to WWI and the fornicating of simple American soldiers with French prostitutes, the Presbyterian president drew a rather selfish line in the sand. We know that from a historian who reported the following:

> " . . . on debarkation at the designated port of St. Nazaire, a dispute with French authorities broke out, after the AEF placed the *Maisons Tolérée* [read "whorehouses"] off limits. With the dispute escalating, President Georges Clemenceau sent a memo to Gen. Pershing offering a compromise: American medical authorities would control designated brothels operated solely for American soldiers. Pershing passed the proposal to Raymond Fosdick, who on giving it to Secretary Baker responded: "For God's sake, Raymond, don't show this to the president or he'll stop the war."[6]

6. This is a verbatim quote from a source I have long since lost. I simply can't be expected to stay on top of such important things while

Wilson promoted killing in the name of the State but was unwilling to promote a violation of the sixth commandment in the name of the State. And, of course, nations often steal the property of other nations in the name of the State and in violation of the seventh commandment (WWI was really about real estate like Alsace-Lorraine, Texas, and Palestine, and had nothing whatsoever to do with the vacuous incantation "To make the world safe for democracy." Woodrow Wilson could not make a single sidewalk in Washington, D.C. "safe for democracy," to say nothing of the entire world). According to such apologists for murder just about anything immoral can be done as long as it is in the name of the State and not conducted at the individual level. One class member made this comforting distinction during the discussion at which revelation I somehow suppressed choking back a challenge.

It should be no surprise, of course, that evangelical churches are full of murderous hawks and very few doves. This has been the case ever since at least 1515 (and long before), when Erasmus wrote

---

being a concert pianist, helplessly trapped in the half-crippled body of an old man, trying to escape it. However, another quote quite similar appears in Meigs, p. 108, and can be seen online at https://books.google.com/books?id=peeuCwAAQBAJ&pg=PA108&lpg=PA108&dq=don%27t+tell+wilson+-or+he%27ll+stop+the+war+baker+clemenceau&source=bl&ots=AWIx-NGDbt&sig=ACfU3U2GyQ-oRatTou_jTIZ_v_Ru8fKog&hl=en&sa=X&ved=2ahUKEwiCgpun8PDoAhWVknIEHeSgDrYQ6AEwAHoECAYKQKQ#v=onepage&q=don't%20tell%20wilson%20or%20he'll%20stop%20the%20war%20baker%20clemenceau&f=false. For even readier reference, see that alternate quote from p. 108 right here:

In a much recounted and revealing incident, French Premier Georges Clemenceau wrote to General Pershing offering licensed and medically inspected houses of prostitution for American Soldiers. While considering the situation, Pershing sent a copy of the letter to Raymond Fosdick [brother of the Baptist heretic, Harry Emerson Fosdick, and president of the Rockefeller Foundation], head of the CTCA [Commission on Training Camp Activities], with instructions to show it to Secretary Baker. Baker read the French suggestion with dismay, saying, "For God's sake, Raymond, don't show this to the President or he'll stop the war!"

There is a lot more in Meigs's book that is very informative about WWI and piece. Prudes should avoid it and retain their naiveté. As for Wilson's relationship with Mrs. Peck, see https://www.americanheritage.com/loveand-guiltwoodrow-wilson-and-mary-hulbert and make up your own voyeuristic mind.

against Christians going off to war, even with Turks and Muslims —if it is true what Laurence M. Vance has to say in his new pamphlet entitled *Erasmus on Christianity, War, and Soldiers*. It is true. Churches routinely celebrate American wars and soldiers in uniform on special holidays, never raising questions about the unjustness of the conflicts like Vietnam which ought to be self-evident to anyone by now. If, of course, such celebrations of Nazi soldiers occurred in German churches today, all hell and Hollywood, insofar as they are different, would break loose in condemnation of the sacrilege. Nevertheless, assuming for a moment the propriety of such honors in totally sinless America, isn't it strange that I have yet to see a church balance things out a bit by honoring peacemakers in a service? The often-damned troublemaking Messiah said in his Sermon on the Mount, "Blessed are the peacemakers for they shall be called the children of God." The only way to save the Savior from fallibility and incoherence is to stress the future tense of his statement: "shall be." Right now peacemakers are generally called Commies, Leftists, and sons-of-bitches; and, as a rule, they have no place whatsoever in conservative churches, where minds are shaped more by the *New York Times* and *NBC* than they are by the New Testament, more by the Pentagon and not the Prophets. God help the poor fellow who challenges the views of Christians immersed in uncritical patriotism. One simply cannot raise the validity of American wars in a discussion because almost every American believes that all of our wars were just by definition.

Sadly even St. Billy Graham did not save us from this myopia. Graham, who knew absolutely nothing about Vietnam and attendant subjects, nevertheless counseled LBJ to bomb North Vietnam, as if he were no different than the pagan Walt Rostow who conducted the war while intoxicated.[7] True it is that Billy saved many

7. Walt Rostow, whose biographer called him "America's Rasputin," was a certifiable war criminal who deserved to be hanged, if Nuremburg rules applied to America after Vietnam. If I had the time during class, I would have told the class about Rostow's intoxication. It so happens that I had friends who knew him. One evening over less dangerous drinks than his, one of them told me how they saw Rostow at a party where he was so drunk that he fell over, face-first, into his plate of food —and then came to and proceeded to eat what his face had fallen into. The mate of my friend corrected him, adding this

souls from eternal torment. It is just as true that he lent his not inconsiderable weight to murdering God alone knows how many more souls —and lost souls at that— with his failure to pay attention to a very simple command in Scripture.

But not every Southern Baptist was afraid of speaking truth to power in matters of war. Rev. J. J. Taylor comes readily to mind, and the class at Green Street Baptist Church needs to know about Rev. Taylor. I hope someone who might read this essay will pass it along, as I still like my crosses padded even after all these paragraphs. Rev. Taylor was once the pastor of the First Baptist Church of Knoxville, Tennessee. Remember that for a moment. Then he moved on to the First Baptist Church of Savannah, Georgia. He was pastoring in Savannah during the days when WWI was breaking out. Rev. Taylor submitted a resolution to the entire Southern Baptist Convention gathered at its annual meeting in New Orleans in May 1917, urging upon his fellow Baptists the meaning of the Sermon on the Mount and that war was no solution. His resolution got 112 votes out of 1,500 cast; and then shortly thereafter he himself was cast out of the pulpit of FBC-Savannah for his pacifism. He should have been hailed to high heaven for his prescience.[8] And he ought to be remembered now in such venues as the Sunday school class from which I just emerged.

Remember that I said that Rev. Taylor had once pastored the First Baptist Church of Knoxville. One of Taylor's successors there

---

nuance: "What Walt actually did was first to vomit onto his plate of food, then fell face-first into it, and then ate it." This is the drunk whom Billy Graham joined in urging LBJ to bomb Vietnam back to the Stone Ages. You won't read this analysis in any of Billy's biographies but only in bombshells like this. And only in footnotes that no one will read anyway because I like to be popular and not stir up hornet's nests.

8. Read a great piece with particulars about J. J. Taylor at https://libertarianchristians.com/ 2015/03/18/man-of-peace/. It is ten times better and more instructive than the Sunday school class that has precipitated these meditations. Or, read it in Appendix E hereinafter, as reproduced with the permission of its author, Laurence M. Vance. Also read the sketch of Taylor by Bill Sumners, the former and now retired Director of the Southern Baptist Historical Library and Archives. It appears in Appendix F hereinafter and appears there with the permission of Mr. Sumners. It was from Mr. Sumners that I first heard of J.J. Taylor, and Bill's revelation of Taylor's life has been revolutionary in mine.

was a fellow named Charles Trentham. When Trentham himself left FBC-Knoxville, he became at FBC-Washington, D.C. the pastor of Jimmy Carter who taught a Sunday school class there. President Carter did not know of J.J. Taylor, Trentham's predecessor back at FBC-Knoxville or at FBC-Savannah. When I sent the story of Rev. Taylor, for a time a fellow-Georgian with the peacemaking Plains peanut farmer, poet laureate, and Sunday school teacher, the president replied that though he was an admirer of Chuck Darwin of *Beagle* fame, he would " . . . give up Darwin's contribution and go with 4004 B.C. in exchange for J.J. Taylor's 'No more war.'"[9] Blessed be Jimmy Carter. And Blessed be me, chicken though I be.

All of this is to say nothing about Franz Jägerstätter, the Austrian peasant farmer who resisted going to war for the Nazis and was beheaded for his decision. See a sketch of Franz online[10] but even better yet see the 2019 movie about his life entitled *A Hidden Life*, trailers of which can be Googled. I first learned of Franz only after the Sunday school class that I attended two months ago and that has prompted this volcanic eruption. I learned of him from the writings of Vernon Grounds, the late president of Denver Seminary and a conservative Baptist who opposed America's entry into WWII. But that is a lesson for another day. The bell has rung and class is over.

9. Letter dated February 19, 2016, from Jimmy Carter to the author.
10. https://en.wikipedia.org/wiki/Franz_J%C3%A4gerst%C3%A4tter.

EXHIBIT A

Alvin York

Sergeant Alvin C. York and Statesman Jimmy Carter: World War I, A World War That Wasn't, and A Movie That Wasn't

SEVENTH EDITION

A Long-winded, Footnoted, Fiery, Seventh-Edition
and Signed Limited Edition Sermon

Preached a Bit Anachronistically on January 1, 1916

(January 1, 2016 is the 101st Anniversary
of Alvin C. York's Conversion to Christianity)

At The First Baptist Church of Schnappsburg*

By its Many-Flawed and Irascible Pastor, Rev. "Jimmy Burns," D.D.

But Dedicated anyway to Glenda and Leonard Smith

(The former who fed his mouth and the latter who fed his mind)

Of the Dillon Road Baptist Church in High Point, North Carolina

And of which Seventh Edition this is signed copy
#_____ of Seven copies

Rev. "Jimmy Burns," D.D.

Texts: Proverbs 16:32 and Ephesians 6:12

"Better is he who rules his own spirit than
he who takes a city"—Solomon

"For we wrestle not with flesh and blood
but with principalities and powers"—Paul

*THE FIRST BAPTIST CHURCH
OF SCHNAPPSBURG

The First Baptist Church of Schnappsburg is a virtual church. It
has no real members; and its quasi-delusional pastor, Rev. "Jimmy
Burns," a bi-vocational pastor/poet/pianist and grumpy old man
who is trapped in a homely coward's body, does not really exist.
However, he does have an imaginary playmate who ghost-speaks
for him and puts his messages in print or online.

Personal vanity is one of the least of the multiplied sins of Rev.
"Burns" for whom the most exciting thing in life is whatever he
plans to say next. However, the Baptist "Burns" could never say in
a real church service half the things he says in his "Sermons from
Schnappsburg" series, as those things would likely get him killed.
He has no martyrdom complex; and his mile-long meandering
motto with a tiny splash of St. Paul's slogan in it is:

> I will not shun to declare unto you between 35–70% of
> the whole counsel of God. The rest of it I am frightened
> to death to declare, and I leave it to others more coura-
> geous than I to quote the Almighty. Unlike the coura-
> geous Sergeant York, Jimmy Carter, William Jennings
> Bryan, J.J. Taylor, Charles Lindbergh, Charlie Bell, and
> others mentioned in the pages to follow, I am a coward
> and I like my crosses padded rather than prickly.

Thus, what you read that follows is probably even watered-down truth as well. Readers are encouraged to use their own best judgment and to ignore the messenger who brought you these meditations—or even to write a red-hot rebuttal to them. Redneck Rev. "Burns" is anything but lukewarm hisself.

The first question I ask myself upon entering a church is, "How can I equip others in attendance right here and right now for furthering the objectives of Jesus as a result of my being present?" Expressed another way, the question is, "How can I give my immediate *ad hoc* neighbors a smile or even the gift of just one small stepping stone right now in this congregational context?" The second question I ask myself is like unto it, viz., "Who here today in this crowd can help equip me for furthering the objectives of Jesus, and how could he/she/they do so?" In short, I don't look at the church as a hotel for saints or as a hospital for sinners but more like a Carolina Panther locker room where one puts on pads for protection and listens to pep talks about eternal touchdowns. In this context one answer to the second question above took place a few weeks ago when I attended a small Wednesday evening supper and prayer meeting at the Dillon Road Baptist Church in Jamestown, North Carolina.

There Glenda and Leonard Smith, two brand new acquaintances of mine, fed me both physically and spiritually. Glenda did the former with the marvelous meals she prepares for those wise enough to have discovered this gold mine of grub in Guilford County instead of looking in vain and in vein for what minerals might be left unearthed in Guilford's nearby McCulloch's Mill; and Leonard did the latter by providing me with a piece of equipment that in spirituality easily exceeds by wide margins at least the last three year's worth of sermons I have heard. And by "three" I mean possibly five, seven, ten, or twenty. And I include my own sorry excuses for sermons in this scathing review.

I refer to a VHS cassette movie entitled "Sergeant York," starring Gary Cooper and Walter Brennan. It is a story about a Christian pacifist (there are Godless Marxist pacifists, too—I knew one once—and thus the "Christian" adjective), Alvin C. York, who lived in East Tennessee but who left those bucolic hills, valleys, and forests full of edible fowl for eastern France in 1918, hungering instead to hunt Huns in the Forest of Argonne near Verdun.[1] The Battle of Argonne, in which York likened his role in the conflict to a turkey shoot back home, was the largest offensive (1.2 million American soldiers) in United States military history. This Battle was in Europe what Antietam was in Maryland during the American Civil War: the bloodiest single day in U.S. history. It is also just as largely forgotten, as are most WWI battles that have been trumped by the far larger images in circulation of its more recent sequel: WWII.

I had a lot of trouble getting into the movie. First of all, our dog Rascal chewed the cover of the movie when I left it on the floor. When I finally fed it into my antiquated machinery, the machine ate the tape. I ordered a brand new one for Leonard, as I did not wish to be remembered for returning something in worse condition than in what I borrowed it. I was afraid, however, to play the brand new tape, as I was afraid my machine would eat it, too. Though a certifiable technophobe, I finally managed to repair the broken tape on my own and put it in another machine late at night. I fell asleep after an hour or so and resolved to finish it the next day. The next day my machine would not even turn on, let alone eat the tape. The next day after that I finally got it on again and would not quit

---

1. I have been to the battlefield at Verdun with my escort and German cousin Matthias. The universally cratered ground much resembles the pockmarked face of someone who had small pox as a child. Stalin's face comes to mind. I have been to many battlefields but this one is utterly unique. The battle lasted 303 days, arguably the longest single battle in history. After WWI the French invested approximately $9 billion to build a wall (shades of China, Israel, Berlin, Mexico, etc.) of fortifications between itself and Germany to preclude this kind of experience from ever happening again. It is known as the Maginot Line. After the French expended the $9 billion to protect Alsace-Lorraine from re-falling into the hands of the Huns, Hitler and his armies simply did an end run around the northern terminus of the Maginot Line and entered Paris. Duh! When I visited the utterly worthless Maginot fortifications, I wondered what would have happened if the French had invested their $9 billion in pastries and shipped them to the Germans as an expression of good will. Obviously there is no way of knowing whether this initiative would have kept the Germans at home in 1939ff. But there is a way to know if it was a better idea. It simply was. It's a no-brainer. Interestingly, the French were once involved in a real Pastry War with Mexico, but that is a totally different story (but one worth Googling).

watching until I had finished it. War movies are hard to watch in more ways than one.

My armchair battle with the tape was well worth it and far better than being in the real battle portrayed in the movie. In short, this movie immediately joined the ranks of my all time favorites which in order are (1) *Les Miserables*, (2) *The Count of Monte Cristo*, (3) *Always*, (4) *Taking Care of Business*, and most recently (5) *Tangerines*, a moving foreign film about war but with English subtitles. The remainder of these mediations will explain just why.

Like York, I am a pacifist of sorts. I am not a complete pacifist, however. I could easily kill and maim babies, pregnant mothers, and old ladies and children; and I could easily waterboard prisoners and nuke my enemies like the Southern Baptist Harry Truman and the best of his bands of brothers from the CIA or other military agencies. My only prerequisite is that I really demand a good reason for doing so, notwithstanding I am generally in short supply of such good reasons. Minister Mark Twain's marvelous "War Prayer" has become my own model mantra for massacring innocents.[2] In addi-

---

2. See www.midwinter.com/lurk/making/warprayer.html for the full text of Twain's "War Prayer." Twain, like the coward "Jimmy Burns," was also a bit of a chicken, as he left his "War Prayer" unpublished until after his death. Twain probably wrote this prayer after America's adventures in the Philippines in 1898. See https://en.wikipedia.org/wiki/Philippine%E2%80%93American _War. For an absolutely amazing consequence of that Philippine adventure, see *The Imperial Cruise: A Secret History of Empire and War* (Little, Brown and Company, 2009) by James Bradley, a highly respected author of books about war in the Pacific and a son of one of the six men photographed raising the flag on Mount Suribachi on Iwo Jima. A dust jacket review of the book states the following: "In 1905 President Teddy Roosevelt dispatched Secretary of War William Taft, his daughter Alice, and a gaggle of congressmen on a mission to Japan, the Philippines, China, and Korea with the intent of forging an agreement to divide up Asia [emphasis mine]. This clandestine and wholly unconstitutional pact lit the fuse that would decades later result in a number of devastating wars: WWII, the Korean War, and the Communist revolution in China." Twain knew what he was talking and praying about. So does Bradley. Interestingly, while Twain's prayer was only a parody, the famous evangelist Billy Sunday actually prayed a real prayer in the U.S. House of Representatives back in March 1918 that is arguably more explosive than Twain's imaginary prayer. It was interrupted three times with the clapping of the Congressmen. It can be seen in full at http://trove.nla.gov.au/ newspaper/article/5538112. It

tion to Twain, in general I subscribe in reverse order to the words of Jimmy Carter, Jim Martin, John the Baptist and Jesus (a Democrat, a Republican, a locust and honey eater, and the son of a carpenter, respectively) when it comes to such potential conflict.

Upon receiving his Nobel Peace Prize, the far underrated and much maligned President/Poet/Peacemaker/Publisher/Peanut farmer from Plains said, "War is sometimes a necessary evil, but it is always evil." Jim Martin, the 70th Governor of the State of North

---

can be seen in part right here:

> We pray that Thou wilt forgive our transgressions and blot out our iniquities. Thou knowest, O Lord, that we are in a life-and-death struggle with one of the most vile, infamous, greedy, avaricious, bloodthirsty, sensual, and vicious nations that ever disgraced the pages of history. Thou knowest that Germany from the eyes of mankind has wrung enough tears to make another sea; that she has drawn blood to redden every wave upon that sea; that she has drawn enough shrieks and groans from the breasts of men, women, and children to make another mountain. We pray Thee that Thou wilt bare Thy mighty arm and strike that great pack of hungry, wolfish Huns, whose fingers drip with blood and gore. We pray Thee that the stars in their courses and the winds and waves may fight against them. We pray Thee that Thou wilt bless our beloved President and give him strength of mind and body and courage of heart for his arduous duties in these sorrow laden, staggering days. We pray Thee to bless the Secretary of War and the Secretary of the Navy, and bless, we pray Thee the Naval Strategy Board. Bless we pray Thee, the generals at the head of our army and the boys across the sea. somewhere in France, and bless those protecting our transports, loaded to the water's edge with men and provisions. Bless our boys at home who are in cantonments. Bless, we pray Thee, this Senate and House, and give them wisdom and strength, for they seem to have come into the kingdom for such a time as this. And, Lord, may every man, woman, and child from Maine to California, from Minnesota to Louisiana, stand up to the last ditch and be glad and willing to suffer and endure until final victory shall come. Bless our Allies, and may victory be ours. And in Thy own time, and in Thy own way, we pray Thee that Thou wilt release the white-winged dove of peace until it shall dispel the storm and clouds that hang lowering over this sin-cursed, blood-soaked, and sorrowing world, and when it is all over we will uncover our heads and lift our faces to the heavens and ring with a new meaning "My country, "tis of thee, sweet land of Liberty, Of thee I sing." And the praise shall come to Thee for evermore through Jesus Christ. Amen.

Carolina, when quoting the poet John Greenleaf Whittier, once said in a speech he delivered in the sleepy hamlet of Whittier in Tar Heeldom, "Peace makes greater demands upon manhood than war." Gung Ho Alpha folks should stop and think about that kind of manhood for a moment before continuing.

(Pause here for a moment to meditate upon Martin's quote).

John the Baptist, when queried by soldiers about their responsibilities, replied, "Do harm to no man, be content with your wages, and do not bear false witness against your enemies." Notice that St. John did not even add, "Oh yes, boys, and leave the virgins alone." More of that remarkable omission in pages to come. And Jesus's words to love one another do not exactly court converts to death penalties—either, not altogether incidentally, in war or in the womb. If it is OK for men to have their way with the bejeweled Woman War, let them at least wage war with these constraints and questions in view—like, "How can I best dispatch this S.O.B in front of me or under me to an eternal hell, *as Jesus would*?" That the Savior would so dispatch some to that everlasting oven there can be no reasonable doubt, if the New Testament is any indication. It is just important to do so in a Christian sort of way.

All this being said, let me pose and infallibly answer the more pointed question, "Was WWI a just war?" Expressed another way, "Was it a "Christian War?" Or, expressed still yet another way, "Did America have any business being involved in WWI?" The short answer is no. The longer answer is an even more resounding no. I shall explain.[3]

3. Many scholars devote a part of their academic lives to the study of just and unjust wars. One of them is Dr. Daniel Heimbach at Southeastern Baptist Theological Seminary in Wake Forest. Heimbach so bathed the brain of George Herbert Walker Bush with this balm in respect to Gulf War I, concluding that it would be a just war. But, in short, the only thing just about it was that it was just a bad war, Heimbach's holy hallucinations notwithstanding. Borrowing Daniel Heimbach's own logic, Herr Hitler might well have argued that WWII was also a just war from the German perspective as a response to the universally-agreed cruel terms of the Treaty of Versailles. Though Hitler blamed Woodrow Wilson's hell-inspired treaty on a conspiracy of Jewish bankers out to plunder the Hun's homeland, American politicians took no chances after WWII in allowing such perceptions to gain ground in the minds of anyone after FDR's Secretary of the Treasury, Henry Morganthau, came up with a plan

President Woodrow Wilson told America that the U.S. entrance into WWI was "to make the world safe for democracy" and was to be "a war to end all wars." Keep in mind two simple things about these statements apart from their transparent and self-authenticating absurdity: (1) Woodrow Wilson had previously been the president of Princeton University where he lost two disputes involving campus real estate.[4] If so ill-equipped to solve such comparatively tiny local problems in Princeton, New Jersey, what qualifications did Wilson bring to solving real estate problems for the whole planet? And, (2) Woodrow Wilson was unable to make a single sidewalk in Washington, DC, "safe for democracy." Ask any adult Black about that. How, then, was Wilson to accomplish such a herculean political feat for an entire planet of pedestrians?

In short, Wilson's proclamation of the reasons for America's entry into WWI was a window-dressing posterity paper and

---

to do to post-war Germany pretty near exactly what Hitler thought the Jews had done to Germany during and after WWI with the Treaty of Versailles. Thus, the now relatively forgotten Morganthau Plan was rejected in favor of the far better known and wiser Marshall Plan for rebuilding Europe. Interestingly, according to my German cousin, German children know more about Morganthau's Plan than American children do. I know that I never heard of Henry's anti-historical hallucinations until I was nearly 60 years old.

4. See Wikipedia article on Wilson from which the following is abstracted: During his time at Princeton, he attempted to curtail the influence of social elites by abolishing the upper-class eating clubs. He proposed moving the students into colleges, also known as quadrangles. Wilson's Quad Plan was met with fierce opposition from Princeton's alumni. Wilson persisted, saying that giving in "would be to temporize with evil." In October 1907, due to the intensity of alumni opposition, the Board of Trustees withdrew its support for the Quad Plan and instructed Wilson to withdraw it. Not long afterward, Wilson suffered a recurrence of his 1906 ailment; as before, a vacation was prescribed and proved beneficial. Late in his tenure, Wilson had a confrontation with Andrew Fleming West, dean of the graduate school, and also West's ally ex-President Grover Cleveland, who was a trustee. Wilson wanted to integrate a proposed graduate school building into the campus core, while West preferred a more distant campus site. In 1909 Wilson's final year at Princeton began with a gift made to the graduate school campaign subject to the graduate school being located off campus; the acceptance of this condition by the board was a pivotal defeat for Wilson. The national press covered the confrontation as a battle between the elites, represented by West, versus the populists, represented by Wilson.

nothing else. So were Colin Powell's more recent and ridiculous declamations about Iraq's weapons of mass destruction on behalf of one evangelical "W," the Second Coming of Woodrow Wilson, who quite creatively said to an aide prior to proof of such weapons, "F—- Saddam! We're taking him out!"[5]

Though Wilson's expressed reasons for American involvement in Europe's affairs are demonstrably false—and, therefore, in violation of the proscription of John the Baptist about using falsehoods in the prosecution of war—Wilson and John the Baptist were probably on the same page sexually. Though the locust and honey-eating prophet did not directly and expressly warn soldiers away from women in their conduct, there can be little doubt that he would have opposed such.

So seems to be the case with the ostensibly pious Presbyterian president, even though some historians are not so sure that Wilson did not have such affairs with one Mary Peck. Other historians are not so unsure and are convinced that he did peck her. I sort of side with the latter in my profession. Whether he did or didn't, at least outwardly Wilson opposed such liaisons. We know that from an offer extended to Wilson by the French statesman, Georges Clemenceau, to supply American soldiers with women upon their entry into his country. Clemenceau extended the offer of medically pure prostitutes to Wilson through General Jack Pershing. Pershing passed the proposal on to Raymond Fosdick, an administrator of the Rockefeller Foundation, who in turn gave it to Wilson's Secretary of War, Newton D. Baker. Baker responded, "For God's sake, Raymond, don't show this to the president or he'll stop the war." For Wilson it was proper to suspend the commandment of Moses and Jesus against killing, but not the one about copulating, even though one might argue that the commandment of Moses and Jesus only proscribed adultery and not fornication in general. Whatever the

5. Here in a rare display of rhetorical sensitivity and out of deference to a dear conservative Baptist brother who still recoils at the full spelling of W's voicing of his synonym of preference for fornication, I have deleted three letters of the F-bomb in the text and six letters from the following reference to the f———quote, the documentation for which is somewhere in *Time* magazine; but I don't have the time to look it up. Trust me. It's there. But try this: https://www.dailykos.com/stories/2004/4/18/24651/-.

case, Wilson at least outwardly opposed both sexual practices but
not the commandment about killing.[6]

6. For a good example of a soldier who held in check his sexual desires
against German women during WWII, it was once possible to see my sketch of
David Smiley online at USADeepSouth. However, that site is no longer up. You
may receive a copy by requesting one at stjimbow@gmail.com. Furthermore, if
the memoirs entitled *Conversations with Stalin* by one Milovan Djilas are correct, even Uncle Joe did not favor this unfortunate use of women, though he
did understand it. Djilas was the Ambassador from Yugoslavia to the Soviet
Union during the WWII period. In that capacity he went to Moscow in part to
complain to Stalin about certain liberties Red Army soldiers had been taking
with Yugoslavian young ladies that they had liberated during the war—a seemingly remarkable complaint for one free-loving communist to be making to
another in the first place. Stalin, resorting to the Christian writer, Dostoyevsky,
attempted to disabuse Djilas of his naïveté, though he did not try to deter Djilas
from his ideals. Employing the devastating Socratic method of Christ (or else
the pre-Christian era method of Jesus by Socrates) challenging the Pharisees,
Stalin, an old Russian Orthodox seminarian himself, questioned Djilas:

> Yes, you have, of course, read Dostoyevsky? Do you see what a
> complicated thing is a man's soul, man's psyche? Well then, imag-
> ine a man who has fought from Stalingrad to Belgrade—over
> thousands of kilometers of his own devastated land, across the
> dead bodies of his comrades and dearest ones. How can such a
> man react normally?
>
> And what is so awful in his having fun with a woman after
> such horrors? You have imagined the Red Army to be ideal. And
> it is not ideal, nor can it be, even if it did not contain a certain
> percentage of criminals—we opened up our penitentiaries and
> stuck everybody into the army.
>
> There was an interesting case. An Air Force Major had fun
> with a woman, and a chivalrous engineer appeared to protect
> her. The Major drew a gun: "Ekh, you mole from the rear!"—and
> he killed the chivalrous engineer. They sentenced the Major to
> death. But somehow the matter was brought before me, and I
> made inquiries—I have the right as commander in chief in time
> of war—and I released the Major and sent him to the front. Now
> he is one of our heroes. One has to understand the soldier. The
> Red Army is not ideal. The important thing is that it fights Ger-
> mans—and it is fighting them well, while the rest doesn't mat-
> ter." Quoted from *The Ballad of Salvation Bill by Robert Service*
> (Jamestown: Schnappsburg University Press, 2008), p. 70.

Pay special attention: In Stalin's ideal world, men would not do such things.
So even the Soviet Premier and the U.S. President were on the same utopian
page. For the Baker quote, see footnote #19 and also Meigs, p. 108..

The real reason for America's entry into WWI was real estate, a field in which Wilson was demonstrably ill prepared. And the real estate in question was Texas, more about which in a paragraph or two to come. For many years and to some degree even still, the sinking of the *Lusitania* on 7 May 1915 has been hawked as the flashpoint that brought America into the war, notwithstanding that the Germans had openly warned that ship that it might be shelled for carrying contraband. And the Germans were correct. The *Lusitania* contained weapons headed for its enemies and it was headed to those enemies with American connivance. What the sinking of the *Lusitania* really did was simply to exacerbate Christian(?) America's hatred of the Germans. It was a platinum-plated propaganda pitch for the Pentagon before it was even built. Additional contributing factors to this growing hatred of the Huns were newspaper articles that spouted ridiculous stories about the Germans not only killing babies but crucifying them! Yes, crucifying them! Shades of Herod and the baby Jesus. For shame.

Interestingly, one such contributor to these kinds of fabrications, properly damned by John the Baptist, was one J. G. de Roulhac Hamilton, a man whose name most North Carolinians do not know and whom even fewer Americans know. Hamilton was the founder of the fabled Southern Historical Collection at the equally fabled University of North Carolina at Chapel Hill. The Department of History at UNC is housed in a building named after Hamilton. If UNC had a Department of Fables—and it probably does, even though it is called the Department of African-American Studies or something akin thereto, where many Black athletes in recent years received credit for attending shell classes—it could just as easily be named after Hamilton who, though he preserved a lot of invaluable history, also helped to peddle a lot of myths less credible than *Alice in Wonderland, Rapunzel,* and *Rumpelstiltskin* all rolled into one.[7] Hamilton and others like him were in explicit violation of

7. In the past year (2015) the fabled University of North Carolina in Chapel Hill has taken many hits for offering a phony class designed to help athletes stay eligible. The subject field was African American history. However, there is a major irony overlooked by the media. UNC once had a Black female professor named Trudier Harris to whom it paid $147,000 per year to teach what

the command of John the Baptist not to bear false witness against one's enemies. So is everyone who employs atrocity fictions for the furtherance of war aims.[8]

Thus, so was the famous baseball player and evangelist, Billy Sunday, who walked one of Woodrow Wilson's own versions of a sawdust trail and converted from Christ to conflict, from wrestling just with principalities and powers to wrestling with real flesh and blood. Lots of blood. Sunday was the preaching predecessor of Billy Graham (who years later experienced an identical conversion from Christ to conflict in Vietnam) and a fellow preacher in whom I myself have religious roots. Billy boarded Wilson's bandwagon for battle against the Germans early on; and, unlike Jesus in re: Pontius Pilate or St. Paul re: Nero or St. John the Divine re: Domitian, the evangelically-sainted Sunday used his famous 1917 revival in New York City as a recruitment station for young men to go to war to the death against dictatorish Deutsch dragons instead of fighting the devilish ideological doctrines of seven-and-ten-headed apocalyptic dragons. In the final analysis, Billy Sunday—whose ancestors were Germans and whose last name symbolized a day of rest—may ultimately have sent more men to hell than he did to heaven. We will find out at the Last Judgment where we might also discover that some of Billy's own Berlinish ancestral kin bit the dust because of his hell-fired hallucinations about the Huns.

---

was advertised as history. One of the topics about which Trudier has written involved a real live mulatto lass named Emily D. West. Careless scholars and amateurs have unhistorically, hilariously, and erroneously equated Emily D. West with an almost certainly fictional and non-existent "Yellow Rose of Texas." Harris is among them. In an irony of ironies, one might argue in defense of the fabled UNC that by offering phony classes involving no study that such athletes were actually further ahead in scholarship at the end of a semester than if they had taken one of Harris's classes.

8. Another recent example of an atrocity story, one designed to exacerbate world hatred toward North Korea, is a story online and repeated by major U.S. media networks that Kim Jong-un had his uncle stripped naked and then executed by turning 120 starving hunting dogs on him. While it sounds to me a bit like something the CIA would do, I am not so sure the North Koreans would stoop that low. See among other sources http://worldnews.nbcnews.com/_news/2014/01/03/ 22156917-kim-jong-uns-executed-uncle-was-eaten-alive-by-120-hungry-dogs?report?lite.

I return to the real reason for America's entry into WWI. It was Texas. The short story is this. In 1917 Mexico was (and still is even in 2016) a bit rankled about how Texas was plucked from its possession by U.S. Congressman, Davy Crockett and Company, back in 1836, and thereafter becoming an American State in 1845. The old adage, "Nothing is ever settled until it is settled right," comes to mind here. Germans familiar with this gargantuan real estate grievance came up with the idea of telling Mexico if it entered the war against the United States, effectively creating a second front for Wilson to deal with (just as the Germans had with France on one side and Russia on the other side) that Germany would restore Texas to Mexico, if Germany won the war. The Texas to which the Germans referred was not just what most Americans picture today as the familiarly-shaped Lone Star State but pre-1836 Texas which also included New Mexico and Arizona.

This message was to be communicated to the Mexicans by way of what is known as the Zimmerman Telegram. The telegram contained a memo about this proposal from Arthur Zimmerman, the Foreign Secretary of the German Empire, to Heinrich von Eckardt, Germany's Ambassador to Mexico, on January 11, 1917. The British intercepted the telegram and, delighted with the prospect of U.S. assistance in pulling their chestnuts out of the fire, passed the information on to America.

Thus, on April 2, 1917, one day after April Fool's Day but a day just as foolish as the former, Woodrow Wilson asked Congress for a Declaration of War against Germany. On April 6, 1917, a day still no less foolish than the first day five days prior to it, Congress complied with the Presbyterian president's unchristian cockamamie and the U.S. formally entered WWI. Mrs. Crawford Toy, the delusional spouse of a Harvard professor, Crawford Toy, had actually believed that Wilson would someday usher in the fabled Kingdom of God foretold by Jesus. She told WW so in a letter. I can't be sure she was bright enough to recognize that after all was said and done that Wilson did not do so. If WWI was the Kingdom of God, maybe we need to give hell a chance.

Not everyone thought Woodrow's declaration of war was a good idea. Many thought there were other ways to address America's

differences with Germany. Among them was one of fundamentalist Christianity's best friends, William Jennings Bryan. Bryan was
Wilson's Secretary of State. He is far better remembered today for
his opposition to Clarence Darrow during the 1925 Scopes Mon-
key Trial in Dayton, Tennessee (roughly 100 miles down dirt roads
from Pall Mall, Tennessee, where Alvin York lived and whose house
is now an historic site open to visitors), than he is for his resignation
as Wilson's Secretary of State. In point of fact, Bryan resigned on
June 9, 1915, almost two years earlier than the sending of the Zimmerman Telegram and two years before Alvin York was drafted,
because he opposed Wilson's warpath toward Berlin. Bryan wrote
the following positively precise prophetic words to warmonger Wilson, his fellow Presbyterian:

> It is not likely that either side will win so complete a
> victory as to be able to dictate terms, and if either side
> does win such a victory it will probably mean prepara-
> tion for another war. It would seem better to look for a
> more rational basis for peace.[9]

The Presbyterian populist, prohibitionist, and presidential aspirant
himself could not have been more prescient. The Treaty of Versailles
did exactly that.

Prescience, however, did not save Bryan from what turned out
to be his own uncritical patriotism. Following Wilson's declaration
of war on April 6, 1917, Bryan reversed field and succumbed to
Woodrow's war fever. In April 1917 he wrote the president again,
this time offering his services. The former pacifist penned his new
position as follows:

> Believing it to be the duty of the citizen to bear his part
> of the burden of war and his share of the peril, I hereby
> tender my services to the Government. Please enroll me
> as a private whenever I am needed and assign me to any
> work that I can do.[10]

9. https://en.wikipedia.org/wiki/William_Jennings_Bryan.
10. https://en.wikipedia.org/wiki/William_Jennings_Bryan.

Wilson, however, did not allow the 57-year-old Bryan to rejoin the military, and did not offer him any wartime role. Eight years later Bryan went to war against Darwin and Darrow in Dayton, Tennessee.

It should not be surprising that the flip-flop of a famous fundamentalist such as Bryan would provide a parallel and precedent for the flip-flop of a far younger fellow from Pall Mall, Tennessee. Though according to the movie Alvin C. York was a horse-riding hell-raising hootch-inhaling hoodlum in the hills of East Tennessee, on January 1, 1915, he underwent an evangelical conversion at the Church of Christ in Christian Union. This was his mother's church and it was pacifistic in tendency, having originated in 1864 in opposition to the Civil War and in opposition to the support of slavery by its parent church, the Methodist Episcopal Church South. Thereupon in the movie, if not in reality, York began to teach a Sunday School class of boys in the church. York taught those boys, "Thou shalt not kill" which, of course, by almost universal religious consent did not apply to all the feathered fowls that flew in Alvin's restricted airspace and occasionally landed on his mother's dining room table—fowl that would presage his fight with the Germans. Stay tuned.

On June 5, 1917, two months after Wilson's Declaration of War, the then 29 year-old York registered for the draft, as was required of all men between the ages of 21 and 31. Still believing in the biblical message, "Thou shalt not kill," the relatively new convert registered as a conscientious objector. His claim was denied. He appealed. Then he was drafted in November 1917 and reported to Camp Gordon in Georgia. There he discussed his pacifistic views with Major Gonzalo Edward Buxton, his battalion commander and a man who was also a Christian but not a pacifist. Buxton sent Alvin back to Pall Mall for ten days to think over the subject after which York returned to Buxton, born yet again, this time for battle in Caesar's army.

Thus, Alvin ended up in France where on October 8, 1918, a month-or-so shy of the Armistice, he captured 132 German soldiers during the Battle of Argonne Forest. For that remarkable achievement he was subsequently awarded a Congressional Medal of Honor and many military honors from other nations. French

Field Marshall Ferdinand Foch told York "What you did was the greatest thing ever accomplished by any soldier by any of the armies of Europe." That's not a bad bouquet, as battle bouquets go. Keep that image in mind for when we get around to spiritual soldier/statesman Jimmy Carter and his averting a holocaustal WWIII and potentially millions of casualties by which teaser I have just given away the store. But keep scrolling down nevertheless.

When York returned to America, numerous financial offers came his way. He declined them, honorably refusing to profit from the carnage in which so many of his own comrades had died not only without any profit but with huge losses. However, he did consent to an autobiography entitled *Sergeant York: His Own Life Story and War Diary* and edited by an Australian named Tom Skeyhill. The book carried a Preface by Newton D. Baker, the same Newton Baker who refused to inform Wilson of Clemenceau's offer of clinically clean prostitutes to American soldiers. And the decorated Tennessean also consented to a movie about his life. It is the movie that Leonard Smith loaned to me one night at the Dillon Road Baptist Church, a church that, quite incidentally, York's third cousin, Joyce Saunders, attends. According to one online source the movie about York was the highest-grossing movie of 1941.[11]

It is important to note one more fact here before proceeding further about Sergeant York's participation in this conflagration. That is that Europe's entry into WWI was no more honorable than America's entry into it over the potential return of Texas to Mexico. In Europe the provocative real estate issue was a large piece of property in France called Alsace-Lorraine. My own physical ancestral roots are in this region where there is even a town having my last name (and here I am speaking of James Lutzweiler, the imaginary playmate of "Jimmy Burns." No one really knows or even cares where "Burns" was born). In 1870 the Germans had swiped Alsace-Lorraine from France, whereupon the last name of my ancestors was changed from the French sounding "Loose-val-eer" (which means "Louisville") to the Germanicized "Lutzweiler" (which also means "Ludwig's Hamlet" or "Louisville"). All of these meditations

---

11. https://en.wikipedia.org/wiki/Alvin_C._York.

above and beyond suggest that Cassius Clay, of whom more to come, is not the only "Louisville Lip" loaded for bear.

In short, then, the French wanted this real estate back; and, understandably so, as Alsace-Lorraine, like Texas, is beautiful. According to Robert L. Owen, a U.S. Senator from Oklahoma and a political ally of William Jennings Bryan, in his remarkable book entitled *The Russian Imperial Conspiracy, 1892–1914: The Most Gigantic Intrigue of All Time*, WWI is rooted in nothing other than a conspiracy between France and Russia to get Alsace-Lorraine back from the Germans for France and to get a warm water port for Russia through the Straits of Bosphorus. In the process the plan was to blame the whole imbroglio of what turned out to be WWI on Germany. It worked, if the abundant words and works of historians since November 11, 1918, are any indication.

And so lust for Alsace-Lorraine, not threats to Pall Mall, Tennessee, is why Sergeant York was in the Argonne Forest fighting Germans on October 8, 1918. He and his battalion were there to help pull French chestnuts out of the fire and not the chestnuts and black walnuts back in Pall Mall. Alvin was not there to make the world or even some of its subdivisions like France or Germany or England or Russia safe for democracy. Neither was he there as a part of a war to end all wars. Ironically and in point of sad fact, this war would not only not end all wars but breed many more Molochausts including not only WWII but the Korean War, the Vietnam War, and all the wars over Palestine since 1948 to name just a few.

Alvin C. York was simply there in the Argonne Forest over someone else's real estate deal gone bad, and he did not even have a dog in that fight. He wasn't alone. Not one American soldier had a dog in that fight including my great Uncle Bill who ingested mustard gas in the battle.[12] Woodrow Wilson and Company were there for the primary purpose of collecting the scraps of real estate that

---

12. Though gassed, it was not mustard that eventually killed Uncle Bill. It was tobacco. I got a Schwinn bicycle out of his death, as he left me in his will for $50.00. That sum would do the trick in the 1950s. It is the first time I was ever left in a will and it was very exciting. At present an old college classmate has included me in his much larger will. I have advised him to go on a heavy salt diet. If he takes my advice, I might be able to write more sermons.

would soon be falling from the tables of the losing belligerents of WWI into the greedy hands of those who would meet in Versailles in the months ahead to divvy up Germany's properties and what was left of the Ottoman Empire (part of which was Palestine, for example, which began right then and there to become the tinder box it is today and probably will forever remain in spite of vacuous everlastingly shop-worn words about a red-herring want for peace). The Treaty of Versailles, created in that fabulous French palace, did exactly what William Jennings Bryan had prophesied in 1915 that it would do, to wit, bring about another war: WWII and the others in its wake to be exact.

Sergeant York recognized this same fact of the futility of his experience in France, but it was only after WWI and not before it. His miniature Pall Mall Church of Christ in Christian Union would have warned him about participation in it on the basis of mere principle alone, not just hindsight. Nevertheless, the farm boy from deep in the mountains of East Tennessee is readily to be forgiven the failure of his foresight; for in 1917 even the entire Tennessee-based quasi-cultured comparatively mammoth Southern Baptist Convention half-crucified Rev. J. J. Taylor of Savannah's First Baptist Church for bringing resolutions before that body expressing hesitation about America's entry into the French fray—after which the war-fevered folks at FBC-Savannah fired him.[13]

And so though York had originally come to believe in the morality of America's intervention in WWI, by the mid-1930s he looked back at that action more critically. He said, "I can't see that

---

13. See an all-too-obscure essay about J.J. Taylor entitled "Joseph Judson Taylor, Pacifist and Anti-evolutionist: Biblical Literalism at its Best" by Bill Sumners. Bill is the Chief Archivist of the Southern Baptist Historical Library and Archives in Nashville, Tennessee. I have a copy in my possession. Readers can secure one from me at stjimbow@gmail.com or by writing to Bill at bill@sbhla.org. There is also some good information in a history of FBC-Savannah by George Shriver. Obscure thanks to FBC's telephone receptionist, Faye Anderson, for scanning and sending to me the relevant pages. What none of these sources note is the very interesting fact that prior to taking on the pastorate at FBC-Savannah, J.J.Taylor had been the pastor of FBC-Knoxville, Tennessee. One of Taylor's later successors at FBC-Knoxville was Rev. Charles Trentham who ultimately moved on to become the pastor of FBC-Washington, DC, where from 1976 until 1980 he was the pastor of President Jimmy Carter.

we did any good. There's as much trouble now as there was when we were over there. I think the slogan, 'A war to end wars,' is all wrong." Though he fully endorsed American preparedness, he still showed sympathy for isolationism in saying he would fight *only* if war came to America.[14] I could do that myself.

But then after arriving at that conclusion, Sergeant York, like any of us understandably confused over what constitute just and unjust conflicts, pacifism and patriotism, was born again again (sic). On Memorial Day in 1941, after already having questioned the validity of WWI, as he did above and in this same year in which the movie about his life grossed more than any other movie, the one-time Pall Mall pacifist praised FDR's support for Great Britain (whose chestnuts Churchill chugged to Newfoundland in August 1941, to beg FDR to help pull out of the fire) in an address at the Tomb of the Unknown Soldier. In that speech Sergeant York now attacked the isolationists, for whom he had previously expressed sympathy.

There at the famous tomb he said that veterans understood that "liberty and freedom are so very precious that you do not fight and win them once and [then] stop." He added that they are "prizes awarded only to those peoples who fight to win them and then keep fighting eternally to hold them!" At times he was a bit belligerent, saying, "I think any man who talks against the interests of his own country ought to be arrested and put in jail, not excepting senators and *colonels* [emphasis mine]." Everyone knew York's colonel in question was Charles Lindbergh who for years fought against America's entry into the foreign fray.[15] But anyone with a clear mind knew infallibly then and even more infallibly since then that Lindbergh had not only not talked against the interests of America but had put America's interests first. A no brainer.

Lindbergh, like Bryan before him and even like the Alvin York of January 1, 1915 through June 5, 1917, both of whom opposed WWI, was also probably right about America avoiding entry into another European War that on December 7, 1941, became WWII. That is a totally different story and this is not the place to get into

---

14. https://en.wikipedia.org/wiki/Alvin_C._York.

15. All of these quotes come from the same source: https://en.wikipedia.org/wiki/Alvin_C._York.

it, as the expression and defense of that viewpoint requires a great deal of discussion about which its proponents have an enormous propaganda head start. Suffice it to say that Jake Cooper, a dear but now dead Jewish friend of mine and a former bodyguard of Leon Trotsky, spent a year of his life in a federal penitentiary in Sandstone, Minnesota, in the early 1940s for his opposition to America's entry into WWII—a good part of which war was designed to save his own blood kinsmen;[16] and suffice it to say that one Arthur McCollum, a Japanese-speaking son of Southern Baptist missionaries to Japan, once wrote a memo for the tendentious eyes of FDR on how to maneuver Japan into firing the first shot in order to precipitate America's entry into the war that Winston Churchill coveted for America to enter like a teenager in heat.[17] All of which is to say nothing of the fate of my ministerial colleague, Rev. Charlie Bell, of the First Baptist Church of Anniston, Alabama. Bell was fired from his position as pastor of that church simply for praying in his pulpit for German soldiers—whereupon he was banished to the pulpit of the First Baptist Church in the Soviet Socialist Republic of Madison, Wisconsin.[18] I relate these three vignettes here merely as teasers to

16. Ironically—and amazingly—Leon Trotsky, a Jew (whom American spy, Raymond Robins, once called "a four-kind son-of-a-bitch but the greatest Jew since Christ") lent aid to the Germans who were killing and concentrate-camping his own kinsmen, all because he wanted the Germans to whip the Soviets so he could return in triumph to that country and "liquidate" Uncle Joe Stalin who had ousted him from power. But in 1940 Stalin beat the traitor Trotsky to the punch—or should I say beat him to the "ice pick"?

17. See *Day of Deceit: The Truth about FDR and Pearl Harbor* (Free Press, 2001) by Robert Stinnett. See also an unpublished sermon by James Lutzweiler about Arthur McCollum entitled "Lesser Known Baptists," dated June 2007 and prepared for the *Baptist History and Heritage Society* annual sermon contest. The pitiful sermon did not even place.

18. I owe the sad story of Charlie Bell to my dear but late friend, David L. Smiley, who at the time of the telling of Bell's tale was a retired professor of American history at Wake Forest University. Smiley was also a surviving alumnus of the beaches at Normandy in 1944. Smiley had been recommended to Bell's Madison, Wisconsin, Baptist ministry by William B. Hesseltine, Smiley's world-class professor of American history at the University of Wisconsin. Hesseltine was an Episcopalian who told Smiley that his own Anglican cult had cut a deal with God: "Episcopalians would stay out of God's business, if God would stay out of theirs." It's a deal that seems to be working. The Soviet

provoke readers into pondering whether Sergeant York was right or whether Lindbergh was right about America's entry into WWII. For my part, I'll go with Lindbergh, Jake Cooper, Charlie Bell and the Alvin York of January 1, 1915 through June 5, 1917, not the Alvin York of Memorial Day 1941.

Even though I am a Southern Baptist, and perhaps just a poor and pitiful representative thereof, my own role model for dealing with these understandable tensions between pacifism and patriotism that Sergeant York and countless others have also experienced is the Muslim, Muhammad Ali, a/k/a the real "Louisville Lip." Though a convert to Islam, Ali, whose given name was Cassius Clay after the famed Kentucky Baptist abolitionist and Abraham Lincoln's Minister to Russia, was raised as a Baptist. He professed Baptist salvation as a youngster in his Louisville church.

Ali's Baptist church was just a couple miles down the road from the flagship seminary of the Southern Baptist Convention. Since all the Holy Ghost power of that school was unable to get the young black boy, Cassius Clay, a cup of cool water in a department store one hot summer day in that otherwise well-watered Ohio Riverfront city, the famed fighter eventually opted for another religion. In 1967, while reigning as the Heavyweight Boxing Champion of the World, the fearless fighter from Alvin York's neighboring state, refused induction for service in the Vietnam War, stating for his reason—and a very good reason—"No Viet Cong never called me 'nigger.'"[19] Clay chose to choose his own enemies rather than let LBJ or LBJ advisor, Walt Rostow,[20] or the president's pugilistic Pentagon

nickname for Madison in the text is Smiley's creation.

19. https://www.nytimes.com/2016/06/06/opinion/muhammad-ali-in
-vietnam.html.

20. Walt Rostow was a certifiable war criminal in the employ of LBJ during Vietnam. His sins are reasonably well known and are becoming even better known after exposés like David Milne's book *America's Rasputin: Walt Rostow and the Vietnam War* (Hill and Wang, 2008). Not as well known is a story about Rostow, who had the power of death over my own young life during the Vietnam era, that is one told to me by one who knew him and who partied with him. My friend, let us call him Hank, was one of the prospects LBJ considered for the writing of his biography. Said Hank to me one day, "I was at a party with Walt Rostow. He was such an alcoholic that at one point he fell

pick his enemies for him. That's not a bad paradigm for a personal decision.[21]

There was no law precluding Sergeant York's proleptic invocation of the same logic as Muhammed Ali with regard to WWI or WWII, as in 1941 the Germans were not threatening to invade either Pall Mall, Tennessee, Louisville, Kentucky, or America at large. He could have protested, "I have no bones to pick with Kaiser Bill." And in point of fact, the Kaiser and his Germans were doing all they could in 1941 and the years leading up to it to avoid America's entrance into the war. It is no accident that the movie about Sergeant York's life came out in 1941, a year in which FDR was attempting to do all he could to overcome isolationism until his coveted attack upon Pearl Harbor did that trick. There can be no question but that Hollywood, too, came to the rescue of Hyde Park, New York's native, FDR, in his scandalous and successful aspiration to be a war president. The movie is enough to make one mindlessly enlist for a war even seventy-five years after its release. I felt a bit like doing so myself, and I am 69 at this writing.

---

over face-first onto his plate of food." Here Hank's spouse corrected him, one otherwise fabled for his Pulitzer Prize-winning precision, by saying, "That's not exactly correct, Hank. First Walt vomited onto his plate of food, then he fell face-first into it—and then he lifted his head back up and ate it." Such is the man who sent multiplied thousands of U.S. soldiers to their deaths in Vietnam and God alone knows how many Vietnamese even though, understandably, Vietnamese lives aren't worth as much, if anything. And, admittedly, being drunk at a party is no crime. Conducting war while intoxicated is or at least should be.

21. Though Muhammad Ali abandoned the Baptist church he had grown up in, he did not altogether abandon the Bible he had embraced as a child. My friend, Gerald Primm, once bumped into Ali in the Cincinnati airport during a stopover for both of them. Gerald, a very conservative Baptist preacher, introduced himself to Ali and asked him for his autograph. The paper Gerald handed to Ali for his autograph was a Gospel tract designed to save him. Ali opened it and scanned it. His eyes fell on some lines in it and then his fingers fell on those lines—fingers that had fallen earlier in the faces of George Foreman and Sonny Liston and many others. The lines from Mark 8:36 read, "What shall it profit a man if he gain the whole world and lose his own soul?" While pointing at them, Ali said to Gerald, "That is true." And there you have it: The Gospel According to Muhammad Ali.

In 2006, fully sixty-five years after the movie about Alvin York came out, a comparatively unheard of fellow by the name of Marion V. Creekmore, Jr. published a virtually unheard of book entitled *A Moment of Crisis: Jimmy Carter, The Power of a Peacemaker, and North Korea's Nuclear Ambitions*. If Creekmore's book were made into a movie, as written, it would probably bore the masses to tears—at least the first fifty-four pages of technical but yet very important details in it that I have read so far.

Creekmore's book, however, was not written for the masses; and I doubt that it will ever become a best-seller. But its message is far more for the masses than the movie about Sergeant York, even though his book is written more though not exclusively for specialists. And it is far more dramatic in what it details. In contrast to WWI and the 1941 movie, Creekmore's book is about an even prospectively far worse "World War That Never Was," thanks to the pouncing unprotected upon a nuclear powder keg called North Korea by the Plains peacemaker, poet, peanut farmer, Professor of Bible at Maranatha Baptist Church, and publisher: Jimmy Carter.

One of the many publications of Carter, who leans more toward St. Paul's principle, to wit, "We wrestle not with flesh and blood but with principalities and powers," than toward Pentagonish pugilism embodied in weapons salesmen, includes his delightful novel, *The Hornet's Nest*. *The Hornet's Nest* is a book about the American Revolution, the bloodiness of which many battles he creatively and courageously argues might have been avoided with proper diplomacy. Apparently, somewhere along the line, the now ancient (91 years old) Carter had also read the proverb, "He who rules his own spirit is better than he who takes a city," shortly after the ink capturing that thought had barely dried on the goose-quill-soaked goatskin of the equally ancient King Solomon. Carter was and still is more into the superiority of self-control than perhaps the aspiring carpet-bomber Ted Cruz and his fellow crimes-against-humanity companions appear to be. At least innocent folks in Teheran, Seoul, and Pyongyang can be grateful for Carter's baptism by Solomon as well as by Southern Baptists like Clarence Jordan of *Cotton Patch Gospel* and *Koinonia* fame instead of by an evangelical like Cruz.

The jury is still out, but probably not for long, on the judgment of the Persian-carpet-crazy presidential contender.

In all events, "The World War That Never Was" refers to a pre-neutralized conflict in 1994 between North Korea, South Korea, and a hawkish United States. It had the potential for widening into an imbroglio involving China, Russia and Japan. It easily could have made WWI look like a neighborhood sandlot touch football game and WWII look like a friendly rematch—if, that is, the nuking of 13,000,000 people in nearby Seoul, Korea (thirty miles south of the DMZ), meant anything at all. I think it means exactly that. One nuke alone on Seoul could have broken Nagasaki's and Hiroshima's hold on the *Guinness Book of World Records* for Asians vaporized in one second by a factor of ten to a hundred. This is to say nothing of the casualties in Pyongyang—or Peking or St. Petersburg or Japan or all of the foregoing.

Statesman Jimmy Carter ought to have been the name of a movie made immediately after such a successful salvation of at least a million victims or so, if not all 13,000,000 souls in Seoul. After all, a million saved lives by one imaginative man not even carrying a weapon trumps by wide margins the nevertheless exponentially heroic and courageous action of Sergeant York in singlehandedly saving the lives of 132 Germans. There was and is nothing to keep Hollywood from making a movie pushing such a peacemaking paradigm except for the financial fact that such movies don't make a lot of money. Most people have not even heard of the moving movie, *Tangerines*, that downplays war and hypes healing between enemies. Hollywood simply has a vested interest in war; and so now in addition to "A World War That Never Was" there is also "A Movie That Never Was."[22] There is just a very good and underrated book by Marion Creekmore, Jr. And though comparatively few will read it, multiplied millions have been benefitted by the message in it about Statesman Carter's conduct in the matter of War and Peace, Tolstoy's treatise or other variations thereof.[23]

22. In re: Hollywood and its lust for war, see Hoopes, pps. 57–59.

23. Tolstoy wrote what is in my view an even more interesting book than *War and Peace* (which, when Woody Allen sped-read it, later commented, "I think it's about Russia"). It is entitled *The Kingdom of God is Within You*. It is an

Carter's conventional reward for such Korean creativity by the mindless media is to be continually demonized by it and its fawning adolescent diplomats as perhaps the worst president in American history. Hogwash! Granting a nanosecond for the sake of a stupid argument that Carter was the worst president in American history, as a simple human being out of office he is far better than all the presidents in American history put together—especially including the most recent three, the earliest of whom was not bright enough or courageous enough on his own to defuse this North Korean nuclear dilemma but who in the irony of ironies with his hollow-headed hawks in fact unnecessarily and incompetently exacerbated the tensions.

The most recent (at this writing) purveyor of this kind of nasty review of President Carter was none other than Jerry Falwell, Jr., the Second Coming of his father, on January 18, 2016, during his introduction of Donald Trump who spoke at Liberty University. Falwell, Jr., would have done well to take a page out of his father's book by not attacking Carter who, upon hearing of Falwell Sr.'s criticism of the President for the Salt II Treaty and returning Panama to the Panamanians, suggested that "Jerry Falwell can—in a very Christian way—as far as I'm concerned, he can go to hell.[24]

Jerry, Jr., might do well to make haste and go and do likewise. In the case of the far more serious matter of Pyongyang than Panama, all Falwell, Jr., had to do to avoid straining out gnats and devouring dromedaries, as he did by dissing Carter and praising Reagan, was to call on his native North Korean Professor of Church History, Dr. C. Daniel Kim (my own professor of Church History hundreds of years ago at a sister seminary in Minneapolis), for a lip

---

extended sermon of sorts itself. My copy was published by The Kremlin Press in 1925, in a year and at a place where the ostensibly Godless Uncle Joe Stalin ruled and reigned. I never cease to be amazed at how the U.S. War Department expends efforts to convert conscientious objectors like York to militarism but fails to give equal time to pacifism by making mandatory reading for all draftees, volunteers, and conscripts of Tolstoy's provocative exposition of Jesus's Sermon on the Mount. It seems sort of academically disrespectable. But then again, so is war.

24. https://www.upi.com/Archives/1986/09/12/Jimmy-Carter-to-Jerry
-Falwell-Go-to-hell/4594526881600/

load about this "World War That Never Was." Dr. Kim, though he still cannot beat me at ping pong at age 94 nor could he at 44, fifty years ago, is living proof that North Koreans are beautiful people in spite of what Bill Clinton's childish advisors may have told him back in 1994. And those "nasty" North Koreans still allow Dr. Kim, though unheralded like Billy Graham, back into their Godless "Hermit Kingdom" to preach Christ's coming Kingdom of God. Carter, like Kim, was even able to share the Christian message with the Commie Kim Il Sung. That is the ostensible goal of old Jerry and young Jerry, but something that neither of them nor even Dr. C. Daniel Kim ever have had a chance to do.

In Falwell's introduction of Trump, Junior Varsity Jerry made it a point to lay a lick on the sacrificial Sunday school-teaching Gospel-preaching President Carter, and then by contrast he loved on the star-gazing Jeane-Dixonish Ronald Reagan. Ronnie with his wife consulted horoscopes as well as the Holy Scriptures—and maybe even bumper stickers and coffee cup captions—for God's direction. In this matter, Junior erred in his estimate, either not knowing history or else knowing it and ignoring it. Falwell seems to have forgotten, if indeed he ever knew, that according to many political pundits that had it not been for the Iranian hostage crisis, President Carter probably would have been re-elected. Just exactly why the American people would have freely re-elected "the worst president in American history," the young president of Liberty University did not explicate. Nor to Falwell's dubious credit has anyone else so explicated.

Nor did Junior Jerry mention how Mr. Reagan approached the Iranians prior to the election of November 4, 1980, and offered to cut them a better deal than Carter would cut them, if they waited until he was elected and took office before releasing them. Richard Nixon did the same thing to Hubert Humphrey with reference to Vietnam in 1968. Thus, those Ayatollah-held Americans got to spend another two and a half months in Iranian detention because of the First Star-gazer/Astrologist from Hellywood. Those hostages sort of symbolize what Mr. Reagan did to the rest of Americans upon whom his damage has not yet totally dawned. It may yet, however.[25]

American critics of Carter like Falwell are not alone. One Ruthie Blum, formerly an American but one who emigrated to Israel in 1977, thereby possibly increasing America's average IQ by 5–10 points, has come out with a hell of a book herself. Not surprisingly it is entitled *To Hell in a Handbasket: Carter, Obama and the Arab Spring.* In it, Blum, a former senior editor for *The Jerusalem Post*, mindlessly nukes her nemesis Carter with nasty nouns even after eighteen years of opportunity (since 1994) to digest the significance of "A World War That Never Was" and now even "A Movie That Never Was." That her book has received high plaudits from former US Ambassador to the United Nations, John "Baloney" Bolton, should be enough to warn readers away from her mind-numbing

---

25. An obscure American named Steve Gilley is one upon whom doubts about Dixon's Dutch Reagan have dawned (Dixon in Illinois, not Jeanne the star-gazer). In a letter to the editor of Greensboro's *News and Record* for January 26, 2016, Gilley wrote:

> Republicans talk about President Reagan as if he walked on water when actually he just walked on the middle class.
>
> Do we really need more of this?
>
> Within months of Reagan taking office he ended government-run services for the mentally ill. He cut programs for the lower-middle-class like Social Security, including disability and survivor benefits, Medicare, unemployment benefits and infrastructure spending. His Tax Equity and Fiscal Responsibility Act of 1982 was the largest peacetime tax increaase on the middle class in history. He also raised the gasoline tax and in 1983 he raised taxes yet again.
>
> Reagan is known as a tax-cutter because of what he did for the super-rich, slashing top rates from 70% to 28%.
>
> He raised the debt ceiling 18 times between February 1981 and September 1987, for a 67% increase that tripled the deficit. In 1989 in the savings and loan crisis he bailed out 747 savings and loans with $160 billion in taxpayer money. In 1986 Reagan gave amnesty to 3 million illegal immigrants.
>
> Reagan helped create the Taliban and Osama Bin Lden by training, arming, equipping and funding Islamist mujahidin fighters in Afghanistan.
>
> I say no more voodoo economics, please.

Whether Gilley got all of his statements correct or not I do not know. But he sounds like he is on to something worth exploring.

literary equivalent of rat poison. Blum's blarney, Israeli though not Irish that she be, is exceeded in toxic waste only by her fellow Israeli, David "Hyperbolic" Horowitz, who authored another senseless screed entitled *Jimmy Carter's War Against the Jews*. Apparently Carter's employment of fourteen Jews at The Carter Center in Atlanta was not enough to qualify dimwit David as a real war color commentator, his moldy mantras about Carter having about as much value as five ounces of fly and flea feculence.

I am about done breathing fire, accent on "about." While I can't produce a movie or write a book about "A World War That Wasn't," I can preach a half-baked sermon about such from a safe distance where I shouldn't be shelled too badly. Besides, Jimmy Carter doesn't need my help to redeem his reputation. His reputation stands on its own merits, which just may go a long way toward explaining why the fevered frontal lobes of mindless midgets like Falwell, Blum, Horowitz, and their ilk can't stand the sainted Sunday school teacher. In fact, my sermon could even hurt the Peacemaker more than help him, as it is larded with a bit of bombast here and there, bombast to which he is a relative stranger. But his nanogenarian shoulders are broad and can still handle the faults of a few of his friends including the irascible old cuss, "Jimmy Burns," one pitiful excuse for a pastor.

Immediately above I said I am "about" done, but not done. I wish to address one technical flaw in the movie about Sergeant York. It was pointed out to me by my neighbor, Pete. Pete is a retired rocket scientist. Really. He is a real live rocket scientist, the kind you hear about in the expression, "It doesn't take a rocket scientist to . . ."—or, as one Minnesota Viking offensive lineman was once rumored to have said in the mixed metaphor of all malapropisms, "It doesn't take a rocket surgeon to . . ." (which explains why the Vikings are not in the Super Bowl). But sometimes it does take a rocket scientist to unravel things, and it sometimes helps if the rocket scientist in question is also a sophisticated gunsmith and gun collector. Pete is.

A couple days ago I saw Pete on my way to the mailbox. Still brooding over and pondering the movie about Sergeant York a couple weeks after seeing it, I asked Pete if he had ever seen it. He said he had and then added that the movie had a technical flaw in it. Curious to explore every nuance of the movie, as well as to share some time with a neighbor, I pressed him for the details. He gladly provided them.

There is a scene in the movie where York shoots eight Germans headed straight toward him. Using for a paradigm his method for taking turkeys down in Tennessee, York pulled the trigger on the last of the eight first, then on number seven, and so on until he plugged the first of those eight who were rushing him. He explained his method to someone after the battle, stating that you shoot the last one in line first because if you shoot the first one in line first, then the others run or fly away. Pete noticed in this scene that the pistol Alvin York used in the movie was a German Luger. He so enjoyed the movie that afterward he read York's memoir in which he discovered that York himself stated that the gun he used on this occasion was not a Luger but his U.S. Army issued .45 caliber pistol. What puzzled Pete was why the movie producer inserted a Luger into the equation, especially since York himself had served as a consultant on the movie.

It would appear that one possible answer to this question is that York himself missed it in the screening. Pete theorized that the producers in a praiseworthy but failed attempt at historical precision used a Luger for this scene because a Luger held eight bullets, and they thought that the U.S. issued .45 only held seven bullets in its barrel, forgetting or else never knowing that the U.S. .45 could also hold an eighth bullet in its chamber. And eight bullets, of course, were critical to the replication of this scene. Who would know that except a rocket scientist?

And so it is that Carter's critics, all of them from the fevered and flawed frontal lobes of Father Falwell and his Offspring to the bowels of Blum's bloviations to the addlepated hubris of "Hyperbolic" Horowitzless are to historical precision more like Lugers than the U.S. issued .45s. They could all use a remedial short course about "A World War That Wasn't" and "A Movie That Never Was."

This tiny scorching sermon might be the closest thing they or any-one else will ever get to it.[26]

26. Interestingly, there is a far more pleasant technical error in the WWI Hollywood movie entitled *All Quiet on the Western Front.*" In it, when the soldier Paul Baumer returns home on leave, and hugs his sister, the straps of a modern bra can be seen showing through her blouse. Bras top bullets and battles any day in the field of technical flaws.

EXHIBIT B

Bonhoeffer Sketch[1]

Dietrich Bonhoeffer (1906—1945)

Synopsis: Dr. Dietrich Bonhoeffer, a German Lutheran, was a student of theology; a curate or pastor of churches in Spain, Germany, and England; a Sunday School teacher in Harlem; a fan of Karl Barth, Gandhi, and Adam Clayton Powell; a student of Reinhold Niebuhr at Union Theological Seminary when heretic Harry Emerson Fosdick taught there; the author of internationally known books and, posthumously, *Letters and Papers from Prison*, which in German was originally entitled *Widerstand und Ergebung* (in English, *Resistance and Submission*) but which could just as easily and accurately have been entitled *Mein Kampf*; and an attempted assassin of Adolph Hitler for which failure he was hanged.

Biography: Dietrich Bonhoeffer's short life and theology can best be summed up in two words used by his fellow Lutheran and perhaps foremost admirer, Martin Marty. Marty referred to the

---

1. This sketch and that of C.I. Scofield in Exhibit I are among twenty such sketches I wrote for another book. Eighteen of those sketches were published but these two were censored out. Bonhoeffer and Scofield are two popular subjects in the denomination in question. My hypothesis for their disappearance best remains cryptic and buried here in an obscure footnote. Yet I do believe in censorship. I would be happy to join many others and burn a copy of this very book at high noon in the middle of Time's Square. No problem.

Delphian Dietrich as an "inconsistent pacifist."[2] Those two words are a verbose euphemism for "assassin."

Given the international acclaim from both liberals and evangelicals that Bonhoeffer has received since his death and right up until this moment, it seems almost sacrilegious to include his name in a book about knuckleheads. But there are still many Christians who would prefer to be remembered as half-wits rather than hitmen. Sadly, Bonhoeffer's role in the attempted liquidation of Hitler remains far better known—but far less incomprehensible—than the literature he left behind.

Heresy: Because biographies of Bonhoeffer are plentiful, his heresy deserves more critical focus than what is readily available to students of theology. And yet care needs to be exercised in contemplating his personal beliefs because Bonhoeffer's abstruse prose and poetry were often so ambiguous that he could make the Sibylline Oracles and the Great Sphinx of Giza combined seem as conclusive as an Aristotelian syllogism. How else could such diverse devotees as God-is-dead theologians on one hand and some fundamentalists on the other both claim such a confessing Christian for inspiration? Perhaps he was really a fundamentalist after all.

What is unmistakable was Bonhoeffer's conduct—if actions still speak not only louder but clearer than words. Bonhoeffer was well aware that St. Paul said that "We war not against flesh and blood but against principalities and powers." Bonhoeffer, one-upping Paul, fought against both.

Bonhoeffer's immediate flesh and blood adversary, of course, was Adolph Hitler. Many would agree that Berlin's bomber Bonhoeffer was right on target. Others might ask, "But why Hitler? Why not Stalin? Why not Kaganovich (who, according to his Jewish nephew, killed 20 million Russians)?[3] Why not Mao? Why not Ben Gurion, the ethnic cleanser of Palestinians? Or, why not the WWII creators of the Treaty of Versailles, many of whom were still living?" Just how does one go about selecting the legitimate candidates for assassination? After all, Jesus did not call for the hanging of Herod or the poisoning of Pilate. Paul did

2. Personal exchange with Martin Marty sometime between 1999–2013. Day or night I cannot recall. Marty has written about Bonhoeffer.

3. See Kahan, front flap of dust jacket and p. 15.

not suggest the neutralizing of Nero, who used burning Christians for luminaries, and St. John did not call for the dispatching of Domitian who was no dear brother of believers in apocalyptic tribulation.

Complicating Bonhoeffer's picture even further was the post-apostolic example of Minnesota's Christian Congressman, Walter Judd. According to one of his close friends and confidents, Judd, who was a medical missionary in China pre-1949, gave healing medical treatment to both Mao and Chiang Kai-shek. Did the doctor sin by not pulling the plug on Mao who made Adolph look like a tyro? Unfortunately, Bonhoeffer did not address the selection issue in his writings, something that his admirer Martin Luther King might have wished James Earl Ray had read carefully.

On the other hand Bonhoeffer did war against some principalities and powers. It is just not always possible to tell who they were. His resort to oxymoronic and amorphous expressions like "religionless Christianity" and "the world that has come of age" make it difficult for one to repent, even if one were so inclined. As Peter said that Paul was occasionally difficult to decipher, so Karl Barth found Bonhoeffer's letters full of "enigmatic utterances." And Barth had no room to talk.

Application: Whom would Jesus assassinate? Whom should any of us assassinate? Surely there are those in desperate need of liquidation. And would it not be better preemptively to do so before they kill forty million-or-so? When one nationally known evangelical pastor and believer in Bonhoeffer was asked what counsel he would give, if one of his young sheepish soldiers had come to him for advice about assassinating Hitler, he replied, "I would tell him to ask someone else."[4] That almost says it all.

JAMES LUTZWEILER, *Jamestown, North Carolina, April 6, 2013*

---

4. I am not at liberty to identify this Canadian-born nationally known author and radio preacher from Moody Church in Chicago, but he knows who he is. And I suppose now do you. The comment took place on a sidewalk on our way to Pizano's Pizzeria, fresh from a visit together with Martin Marty. It, too, took place sometime between 1999 and 2013. Pizano's pepperoni pizza is on State Street just down the street from the famous Pacific Garden Mission—where Billy Sunday got saved and about whom Frank Sinatra sang that Sunday could not shut down Chicago including State Street—is the best you will ever eat, and you will never find a more mouth-watering footnote than this in all of literature.

EXHIBIT C

Letter to Quentin Self

14 July 2019

Rev. Quentin Self
Green Street Baptist Church
303 N. Rotary Drive
High Point, NC 27262

My dear young brother Quentin,

I am writing you pursuant to the last thing you said in your sermon this morning at Green Street Baptist Church. I refer to your reference to Dietrich Bonhoeffer as a "martyr." I am wondering if perhaps you might wish to reconsider that honorary noun in the future.

For context in re: this question, I refer you to an essay (enclosed) I wrote about Dietrich Bonhoeffer for a book originally to be entitled *Knuckleheads in Church History* but which was eventually entitled and published as *Churchfails:100 Blunders in Church History and What We Can Learn from Them* (Nashville: Holman Reference, 2016). I also enclose a complimentary copy of that book

Exhibit C

for your stimulation even though it just might be the worst-selling book in American publishing history. And though I contributed eighteen essays in this book, my Bonhoeffer essay was censored out of it by Lifeway's editors, as was another essay I contributed about the certifiable scoundrel/scalawag C. I. Scofield. It would appear on the surface that average Southern Baptist readers were not mature enough to digest the facts and disturbing questions about either clergyman; and I suspect the fact that Scofield has been a best-seller among Southern Baptists might also have had a little to do with the expunging—though perish that temple-cleansing thought. Thus, you really didn't have a prayer of encountering an alternative view about Bonhoeffer from this significant shaper of Southern Baptist minds.

Was Jeffrey Dahmer perhaps a "martyr"? How about Karla Faye Tucker? Maybe Charles Manson? I suspect you would protest the use of this honorable word with respect to them, as would I. However, I think the general reason that Bonhoeffer gets a free pass in this regard is because the object of his selective wrath was the 20th century's poster boy for evil. But then, why not Mao? Why not Uncle Joe? Why not the ethnic-cleanser, Ben Gurion? Where are the priorities, when we need them?

Of course, the striking and disturbing corollary of the characterization of Bonhoeffer as a "martyr" raises the uncomfortable question of who today, right now, Sunday, July 14, 2019, qualifies as a legitimate target for assassination. Would it be Obama? Trump? AOC? Abortionists? Iranaphobes? John Bolton? Bibi Netanyahu? Vladimir Putin (who attends church and is a favorite among Russian Baptists—and yours truly)? In short, whom would you, Pastor Quentin Self, nominate as a candidate not for president but for assassination right now? This minute? Should someone in the Green Street Baptist youth group come to you and tell you that he/she feels a call from God to assassinate someone, whom would you suggest as a *bona fide* target? And would Green Street Baptist Church endorse this selection?

I understand from a statement I heard you make some time in the past that in some context somewhere you were going off to help equip pastors. This brief letter is to help equip you and to help you equip them.

Please equip me with your reply. Please name some names. And without looking, please tell me all you know about Herschel Grynszpan.

Fraternally yours for Christ and His Kingdom,

James Lutzweiler
Archivist (1999–2013), Southeastern Baptist Theological Seminary
336–686-2043
stjimbow@gmail.com

EXHIBIT D

Lesser Known Baptists

A Sermon of 2,378 words

Submitted to the *Baptist History and Heritage Society*

For the Annual BHHS Sermon Contest

June 2007

By

James Lutzweiler

Archivist, Southeastern Baptist Theological Seminary

114 N. Wingate, Wake Forest, North Carolina 27587

919–761-2249 (O) 336–454-0828 (H) 336–686-2043 (M)
919–761-2150 FAX

LESSER-KNOWN BAPTISTS

One major difference between secular and sacred history is what or who we are called upon to remember. As participants in the great democratic experiment we call America, we have been encouraged to "Remember the Alamo!" to "Remember the Maine!" to "Remember Pearl Harbor!" and most recently to "Remember 9/11!" As subjects in the great monarchy we call the Kingdom of God, we have been encouraged first of all to remember people—like Jesus, as if without this commandment we could actually forget him. Others in the Scriptures we are specifically told to remember are Lot's wife, Paul, the poor, and prisoners. In the years that have passed since the ink dried on the first parchment of the *Apocalypse*, there are a few other folks I don't think it would be anti-biblical, even if extra-biblical, to add to the list for remembering. I am thinking, of course, of some Baptists; and, more specifically, of some lesser-known Baptists.

For many years now I have been compiling a list of lesser-known Baptists, a list of folks that at least I did not readily recognize as Baptists or who were at least raised for a time as Baptists. On my list are to be found names like Tom Lincoln and his son Abe; Elvis Presley, Muhammad Ali, Van Cliburn, Louis Armstrong (no relation to Annie), Sam Houston, Dale Evans, Brittany Spears, Jim Brown, Buddy Holly, Joe Frazier, Hank Williams, Gene Autry, Roy Orbison, Clarence Thomas, Tony Dungy, and most recently my new found friend, Ray Stevens—not the singer of the hilarious "Mississippi Squirrel Revival" at the First Baptist Church of Pascagoula but the Southern Baptist past president of Baltimore's otherwise relatively godless H.L. Mencken Society and a donor to Tennessee's Bryan College of a magnificent collection of rare Menckeniana.[1]

Bryan College, of course, is named after William Jennings Bryan of Scopes Trial infamy but lesser known for his far more important World War I peacemaking initiatives. In spite of the claim in six successive editions of a college history textbook I teach from, a book written by two well-known scholars but lesser-known

---

1. More such Baptists can be found at http://www.adherents.com/largecom/ fam_bap.html.

Baptists (one of them the president of Furman University), the great statesman and "Commoner" Bryan was not a Baptist, lesser-known or otherwise. He was a Presbyterian of whom Theodore Roosevelt nevertheless said, "By George, he would make the greatest Baptist preacher on earth."[2] Notwithstanding that Bryan was not a Baptist, he is still worth remembering in these peaceless days that have many of their roots in the very war Bryan fought against.

There is a lot to remember about these lesser-known Baptists I have just named, though, of course, they are not lesser-known people, just lesser-known as Baptists. E.g., Tom Lincoln sometimes paid his tithes with whiskey, a truth revealing that teetotaling has not always been a central theme in Baptist history. Such a fact would no doubt disturb the Baptist preacher who, when reminded by his Presbyterian counterpart that Jesus never forbade alcohol, replied, "Yes, but we Baptists would have thought a whole lot more of him, if he had."[3]

Then there is Elvis Presley who, according to Adrian Rogers, used to slip into the balcony of Bellevue Baptist Church after the service started and left discreetly before it ended. And there is the colorful Sam Houston who, when asked if all of his sins were

2. The authors of the textbook *America: A Narrative History* (New York: W.W. Norton & Company, 2004) is authored by George Brown Tindall, retired professor of history at The University of North Carolina, and David E. Shi, president of Furman University. I use the text in my basic American history course at Guilford Technical Community College in Jamestown, North Carolina. A plausible though unintended explanation for Tindall and Shi's error is provided by Doug Linder at http://www.law.umkc.edu/faculty/projects/ftrials/scopes/bryan w.htm where Linder writes, "A Baptist preacher he [Bryan] might have been, too, were it not for his boyhood fear of water. As a young boy in the 1860s in Salem, Illinois (the same small town in [which] John Scopes studied high school biology), Bryan dreamed of becoming a preacher in the Baptist Church of his father. Witnessing his first baptismal immersion at age six, however, changed his career plans. Bryan later claimed that his fear of water was so great that it led to his decision to leave the Baptist Church and become a Presbyterian at age fourteen." For an up to date look at Bryan by a Baptist see Gerald Priest's essay in the journal of the Detroit Baptist Theological Seminary. It is online at https://drive.google.com/file/d/1PzCQXJ3tLaboRIEGPed OxxLBn8GqEWVu/view.

3. Got this story from an old newspaper clipping now lost. No problem. It is unforgettable.

washed away when he was baptized, replied, "If they were, God have mercy on the fish downstream."[4] I cringe when I think of the little Baptist boy, Cassius Clay, who testified of a conversion in Louisville, where all the efforts of E.Y. Mullins could not get him a drink of water on a hot summer day at a local department store fountain. But I rejoice in the little Baptist church in New Orleans that saved Louis Armstrong who has regaled us all with "What a Wonderful World" and a toothy grin that outdid Davy Crockett and Jimmy Carter combined.[5] And what could I possibly add to what

4. This is the way I remember the quote. It has many variations. See https://www.yourconroenews.com/neighborhood/moco/opinion/article/A-Father-s-Day-lesson-about-Sam-Houston-9282842.php.

5. See Brothers, *Louis Armstrong's New Orleans*. Presley's attendance at Bellevue is told in a letter to this writer from Adrian Rogers. Marquis James tells the story of Sam Houston in his biography of Houston entitled *The Raven*. The story of Lincoln paying his tithes in whiskey is contained in an undated clipping in the author's possession. That Kentucky ministers would accept part of their salaries in whiskey is related in a story entitled "A Baptist Minister Invented Bourbon" which is online at http://www.maysvilleexplorer.com/blog/archives.do?blogid=1&mo nth=2006-8-01. That column reads as follows:

> Since we were talking about the Pogue Distillery yesterday, and since Pogue is famous for its bourbon—in fact, all of Kentucky is famous for its bourbon whiskey—I thought I'd tell the ironic story of how a Baptist minister invented bourbon.
>
> In the frontier woodlands that was Kentucky during the late 1700s, cash and coin was rare and bartering was a common method of doing business. Many ministers were paid tithes in grain, which became a lot of grain. It became more than any church could consume and therefore many of the ministers went into the distillery business. One of these ministers, Elijah Craig, ran a small distillery in what was then called Bourbon County. Elijah Craig was notoriously cheap. One day he had an idea to burn out the insides of the oak barrels he aged his whiskey in so that he could get more use out of them. He quickly found that people seemed to like the flavor imparted by the burnt barrels better than the regular oak aged whiskey, and thus bourbon whiskey was born.
>
> The ironic part is that Baptists later became the champions of the temperance movement and Bourbon County, now called Scott County (just a few counties over from us), has a large Baptist population. The birthplace of bourbon whiskey is today dry as a bone. Although technically a dry county, legend has it that several casks of Elijah Craig's original bourbon were placed

has already been said recently about Tony Dungy except that he is not only a Christian but a Baptist.

There is, however, a lesser-known Baptist who is also a lesser-known person—one might even say a deliberately secretive person—upon whom I would like to focus our attention for a few moments. We need to remember him, as he was very much involved in one of the most memorable episodes in American history. His name is Arthur H. McCollum. It is doubtful that any of you have ever heard his name before today, unless you have read Robert B. Stinnett's sensational book *Day of Deceit: The Truth about FDR and Pearl Harbor* (New York: Simon & Schuster, 2000), a book about which Richard Bernstein of the *New York Times* said "It is difficult, after reading this copiously documented book, not to wonder about previously unchallenged assumptions about Pearl Harbor."[6]

Let me tell you first what author Stinnett says about Arthur McCollum, before I tell you what Stinnett does not tell us about him. Stinnett writes:

> Born to Baptist missionary parents in Nagasaki in 1898, McCollum spent his youth in various Japanese cities. He understood the Japanese culture, and spoke the language before learning English . . . At eighteen McCollum was appointed to the Naval Academy. After graduation, the twenty-two year old ensign was posted to the US Embassy in Tokyo as a naval attaché and took a refresher course in Japanese there. McCollum was no stuffed shirt. He enjoyed parties and the favorite drink of Japan's naval community—Johnny Walker Black Label Scotch. He was never at a loss for words. After telling a long story, he'd pause with his favorite phrase, "In other words," then go into an even longer version.
>
> In 1923, as the fads of the Roaring Twenties swept the world, members of the Japanese Imperial household were anxious to learn the Charleston. McCollum knew the latest dance routines, so the embassy assigned him

---

inside the columns of the administration building of the equally Baptist Georgetown College (which Craig had founded).

6. Bernstein's review appears on the back cover of Stinnett's book.

> to instruct Crown Prince Hirohito, the future Emperor,
> in slapping his knees to those jazz-age rhythms.[7]

Drinking and dancing, if sins at all, were mere gnats next to McCollum's camel-sized crimes against Christ and those for whom Christ died in the days leading up to Pearl Harbor. For it was McCollum, later Lieutenant Commander McCollum of the Office of Naval Intelligence, who on October 7, 1940, submitted a sensational but secret memorandum to two of FDR's most trusted military advisors. It detailed "an eight step plan to provoke Japan into attacking the United States." The memo was not declassified until 1994 and Stinnett is the one who discovered it using an FOIA request rather than waiting for the famously forthcoming federal government voluntarily to share it. In McCollum's exact words, "If by these means [the eight steps he outlined] *Japan could be led to commit an overt act of war,* so much the better." President Roosevelt, over the course of 1941, implemented all eight of the recommendations contained in the McCollum memo. Following the eighth provocation, Japan attacked. The public was told that it was a complete surprise, an "intelligence failure," and America entered World War Two [emphasis mine].[8]

Glenn Hinson, Glen Stassen, and Eiko Kanamaru have all written essays for *BHAH* (Baptist History and Heritage Society) about Japan and the war, but Arthur McCollum has flown under their radar.[9] For that matter he has flown under the radar of the numerous United States Congressional Committees that have investigated Pearl Harbor. He has, in fact, flown under everyone's radar but Stinnett's. But Stinnett's statement that McCollum was born of Baptist missionaries in Nagasaki enables us now to explore a bit more in depth than did he the religious ramifications of this story.

Arthur McCollum was not just born of any old missionary parents but of J.W. McCollum and his wife Drucilla, one of the two pairs of pioneering missionaries to Japan in 1889. Earlier Lottie

7. Stinnett, p. 6–7.

8. The gist of Stinnett's story about McCollum including these quotes can be found online at http://www.whatreallyhappened.com/McCollum/.

9. See Hinson, "Baptist Attitudes Toward War and Peace Since 1914," *B*; Stassen, "Harry Truman as Baptist President;" and Kanamaru, "Japanese Baptists' compromise with nationalism in 1941.

Moon and Crawford Toy had set their sights on Japan, but it was J.W. and Drucilla who laid the groundwork for the Southern Baptist missionary enterprise in Japan—an enterprise that resulted in churches being planted both in Nagasaki and Hiroshima as well as in many other cities.

While Toy never made it to Japan at all, Lottie Moon spent some time living with the McCollums there in 1901 when she escaped for a few months from the turmoil associated with the Boxer Rebellion then going on in China. In a letter dated February 15, 1901 she writes among other things that while in Japan she "was teaching Mr. McCollum's boys."[10] One of those boys would have been Arthur, though at the time he was only three years old and could not have learned much. Nevertheless, he had to know in later years that his life had intersected with this legendary lady. But it is quite clear that Arthur did not learn to love Japan as the Southern-Sino-sainted Lottie loved China. At least it is difficult to visualize missionary Moon composing a memorandum for the United States to provoke China into an attack that would justify a retaliatory strike against the people she was sacrificing her very life for.

Missionary kid McCollum's conduct stands in stark contrast to another MK born in Nagaskai. I refer to Edwin B. Dozier who himself served for many years in Japan with distinction and who wrote several books about his missionary experiences. Educated at Wake Forest College, Dozier also served for a time as a pastor in Hawaii. He was there when the Japanese bombed Pearl Harbor, finding the action incredible. During the previous months he had turned down requests that he work with the American Secret Service in Hawaii, refusing to blend the missionary and military enterprises.[11]

Missionary Max Garrott is another Baptist whose conduct sets McCollum's memorandum in bold relief. Garrott was still Christian soldiering in Japan when Pearl Harbor was bombed. Those "dirty

---

10. Cited in Harper, *Send the Light: Lottie Moon*, p. 303. In a subsequent letter she explained her reasoning for leaving China for the time being. She said, "One is willing to be shot or murdered outright, but [not] to be cut to pieces as was the wife of the Belgian engineer before her husband's eyes," p. 304.

11. See Parker.

Japs" were so cruel to him in his forced confinement there that he later testified of having "had strawberry shortcake running out of [his] ears." When he returned to America as the result of a prisoner exchange, Garrott met with repatriation difficulties from U.S. government officials "because of his conviction that he could not take part in the war effort."[12]

The conduct of both Dozier and Garrott raises some good questions about the age-old Baptist principal of separation between church and state. Surely the God of Baptists does not need the endorsement of either the superpower United States government or superstar athletes to accomplish his work on earth, though he welcomes their worship. But it appears from time to time that our government finds it expedient to tap into the gifts of the church, gifts made possible by other nations putting out a welcome mat for missionaries, to accomplish its less than peaceful purposes. The practice reminds one of the Old Testament proscription of boiling a calf in its mother's milk (Exodus 23:19), whether the author intended the comparison or not. Dozier and Garrott *vis a vis* McCollum stand out as two men whose minds appear to have been transformed more by the prophets than the Pentagon.

Jimmy Carter, not a lesser-known Baptist but still a Naval officer like McCollum, also has been transformed by Dozier's and Garrott's prophetic message of peacemaking. Amazingly, people with ostensibly 20–20 hindsight still blindly criticize the Plains poet and president for not bombing Teheran back into the Stone Age in 1979, notwithstanding the overwhelming evidence and wisdom to the contrary staring all of us right in the face today. More Baptists, both the widely-known and the lesser-known varieties, need to take Solomon seriously when he told his son that it is better to rule one's own spirit than to take a city (Proverbs 16:32), whether that city be Teheran, Baghdad, Berlin—or even Nagasaki and Hiroshima. Fundamentalists who criticize Carter ought to fall on their knees and thank God that there are just that many more Muslims to save in the Mideast because Carter let truth rather than testosterone be his guide. Let us not forget poet Whittier's words, which are true,

12. Parker, p. 165.

60

even if they aren't expressly biblical, to wit, "Peace makes greater demands upon manhood than war."[13]

Arthur McCollum is just one of many lesser-known Baptists that are now clearly in view to remember for better or worse. Another whom I remember and cherish is my late father-in-law, Ken Gibby, from Japan, North Carolina (a hamlet now inundated by the TVA's Fontana Lake rather than a Lake of Firestorm bombing), a Pearl Harbor survivor who keenly stimulated my interest in this subject. And a lesser known Baptist whose memory I just cannot shake is the woman who replaced Lottie Moon as the wife of the well known Crawford Toy. Mrs. Toy was an occasional correspondent of Woodrow Wilson. In one of her letters she told President Wilson that many were looking to him to bring in the Kingdom of God. If what we are seeing today is the Kingdom of God, perhaps damnation is preferable.[14] Wilson's war to end all wars has become a peace to end all peace.

In all of these meditations there are some other lesser-known Baptists whom I am trying to know, even though so far I have come up dry. I keep looking for names to remember of just one or two Baptists from Nagasaki or Hiroshima, Baptists who were unnecessarily bombed to smithereens by their ostensible Baptist brother, Harry Truman. Most Baptists have been more upset over the president's profanity than his projectiles. According to Glenn Stassen in his fine article and Gar Alperovitz in his fireball book, an ever growing number of folks are beginning to doubt the need for that holocaust.

If I could meet such a lesser-known Baptist, I would ask the one from Nagasaki if perchance he or she had as a childhood chum

13.. Cited by North Carolina Governor James Martin in a speech commemorating the 100th anniversary of Whittier, North Carolina, a town named after poet Whittier's cousin. Copy in the author's possession.

14. Mrs. Toy's letter is published among the papers of Woodrow Wilson. A copy of this letter is in the author's possession. The missing volume number and page number are a casualty of cornoavirus because I can't get to the library to certify them, but it is in there. It is also somewhere in the Wilson papers online but will take someone brighter than I to fish it up. But it is worth fishing up. If Mrs. Toy's statement could be alchemized into bait, it would be great catfish bait, as it stinks to high heaven and beyond.

in Sunday School the lesser-known Baptist boy, Arthur McCollum, and father of the adult Naval officer McCollum—if "the boy is still the father of the man"—who used the gifts of his hosts' Japanese language and culture. I want to weep with them and repudiate the resort to the weapons of mass destruction, used first not by Saddam Hussein but by a Southern Baptist.

EXHIBIT E

"J. J. Taylor" by Laurence M. Vance

and used with his permission

Since the beginning of the U.S. invasion of Iraq in 2003, two words
that have rarely been seen together are "Baptist" and "pacifist." We
have instead been subject to things like high-profile Baptist leader
Jerry Falwell writing a defense of the Iraq war titled "God Is Pro-
War," Richard Land, head of the Southern Baptist Convention's Eth-
ics & Religious Liberty Commission, writing to President Bush that
his "policies concerning the ongoing international terrorist campaign against America" were "both right and just," and the Southern
Baptist Convention passing resolutions expressing appreciation for
President Bush, U.S. troops, military chaplains, and the war effort.

I have stood against this nonsense from the very beginning.
At times virtually alone. I recently discovered a kindred spirit in the
Baptist pacifist Joseph Judson Taylor.

Taylor was born in 1855 in Henry County, Virginia. He was
named for his maternal grandfather, Joseph King, who had served
in the Virginia Legislature, and Adoniram Judson, the famous Baptist missionary to Burma who died five years before Taylor's birth.

Taylor attended Richmond College from 1875–1880, earning
his bachelor's and master's degrees. He was chosen valedictorian
for the commencement. He was ordained a minister in 1876. The
Southern Baptist Convention met in Richmond that year, and

Taylor attended the meeting for the first time. He first attended as a delegate in 1881, and was elected vice-president for the first time in 1906. He also served on many denominational committees over the years. He married the college-educated Anna Hinton in 1882. After graduation from Richmond, he attended the Southern Baptist Theological Seminary in Louisville, but never took the examinations necessary to graduate. However, in 1889 Taylor received a Doctor of Divinity degree from Howard College in Alabama (now Samford University), and in 1904, a Doctor of Laws degree from Union University in Tennessee.

Taylor pastored churches in Lexington (1881–1887), Mobile (1887–1899), Norfolk (1899–1903), Knoxville (1907–1915), Savannah (1915–1917), Leaksville, North Carolina (1918–1922), and Jasper, Alabama (1922–1927). During his successful pastorates, he baptized over 1,000 people. From 1903–1907 he was president of Georgetown College in Kentucky. Taylor was a theological conservative. He was an outspoken *proponent* of the literal interpretation of the Bible and the separation of church and state and *opponent* of evolution and modernism. He believed that evolutionary thought was linked to unbelief. He also considered the position of theistic evolution to be "utter and dangerous nonsense." He even published a book against evolution in 1926 titled *Evolution Theory: Plain Words for Plain Folks*. Taylor openly criticized the liberal Baptist Harry Emerson Fosdick for denying the fundamentals of the Christian faith. Like any good libertarian, Taylor opposed state laws that forced businesses to close on Sunday. He also consistently opposed violence, whether it was the lynching of blacks, the death penalty, or war.

It is why Taylor left his pastorate in Savannah that is of special concern. After three days of discussion with Taylor in Knoxville, the pulpit committee of the First Baptist Church of Savannah introduced him to the congregation in glowing terms: "He stands among the foremost of our preachers in a Southern pulpit. In doctrine he is sound, clear, and conservative. As a man he is scholarly, yet genial; aggressive, but prudent; commanding the respect of the world as he wins the hearts of all." All was well and uneventful during Taylor's first two years in Savannah.

The annual meeting of the Southern Baptist Convention was held in New Orleans on May 16–21, 1917. It would probably have been uneventful as well were it not that the United States had just declared war on Germany the previous month and officially entered World War I on the side of the Allies to end all wars and help make the world safe for democracy.

On the first day of the meeting, J. W. Porter of Kentucky offered a resolution pledging the support of Southern Baptists to the war effort:

> *Resolved*, That we, the representatives of 2,744,000
> Southern Baptists in Convention assembled, pledge
> to our President and government, our prayers, our
> loyal and sacrificial support in the war in which we are
> engaged. To this end, we pledge our property, our lives
> and our sacred honor.

A request was made to table the resolution as it was not the proper time to discuss it since the custom of the Convention was "to reject all resolutions and motions that did not bear directly on the work of the body." But Porter was applauded when the said that "he could not conceive of men from the land of Lee and Jackson being opposed to such a resolution." The motion to table the resolution was voted down and the resolution was passed.

Taylor later said that he was at once "impressed with the impropriety of the resolution, and refused the unanimous consent requested." He charged the Convention with violating its own constitution in adopting the resolution, for the purposes of the Convention "certainly do not include the raising of armies and the gathering of funds to wage a carnal war."

On Friday afternoon, Taylor presented to the Convention for consideration a peace resolution:

> WHEREAS, There has come upon the earth a spirit
> which has plunged the nations that have been consid-
> ered foremost in the lines of advancing civilization into
> a war more ruthless and more destructive of human life
> and human happiness than the world has ever before
> known; therefore be it

Resolved,

1. That we deeply deplore the awful and sorrowful calamity which has caused these leading nations to drench the earth in the precious blood of their own loyal citizens.
2. That we affirm our faith in the righteousness of the Sermon on the Mount, and our confidence in the infallible wisdom of him who taught us to love our enemies, to bless them that curse us, and to do good to them that despitefully use and persecute us.
3. That we desire a stronger faith in the God who maketh wars to cease even unto the ends of the earth, and we shall rejoice if our own people, and all of every name who love the Lord Jesus Christ in sincerity, shall find it in their hearts to pray for kings and all that are in authority that we may live quiet and peaceable lives in all godliness and honesty.

The resolution failed with only 112 votes in the affirmative out of over 1,500.

On Saturday evening, the Convention heard a report from the Committee on World Crisis that offered a message for adoption. It read in part:

We cannot close this message without reminding our people that it is their Christian duty in a time like this to support heartily in every way possible the men whom we have called to the leadership of the country. Many of us cannot bear arms, but every one of us can do his part, as, in the providence of God, it is disclosed to him.

It is of special significance to Baptists that the issues involved in the great war concern fundamental human rights and liberties. The cause of democracy is at stake. While we would not voluntarily claim for ourselves any superior devotion to this great cause, yet we cannot forget that democracy is peculiarly a part of our religion, that it is interwoven with all our common and cherished beliefs.

Deeply as all of us deplore war, ardently as we longed and labored to avert or avoid it, we may be cheered and heartened in remembering that we are moved in entering it, neither by lust nor hate, but by the love of humanity.

Taylor opposed the adoption of the message. He "deplored the gloating and hand clapping over human beings being shot to death." He said "the Convention had too much of Caesar and too little of God." Nevertheless, the report was adopted.

Taylor's remarks were branded as "seditious," "unloyal," and "treasonable." The incident was said to be "the stormiest scene that was ever enacted on the floor of the Convention." Taylor wrote later that he was "hooted and hissed and threatened with personal violence by honourable members of the body."

Taylor then returned to his church in Savannah and preached a message titled "The Divided Kingdom" in which he expressed his views on war and peace. He proclaimed that the church "is not called to usurp the place of Congress in declaring war, nor is it appointed to gather arms or even to sell bonds to put money into the national treasury." The church was not "to give formal sanction to the shedding of blood." He publicly argued that his address at the Convention with the presentation of his peace resolution "did not contain one single treasonable or disloyal utterance." He expressed in an August 1917 letter his objection to the church in which he belonged "taking formal part in this orgy of butchery and blood."

Because Taylor's "pacifism" was at odds with the church's support of the war effort, the breach between the pastor and the congregation only widened. At a deacon's meeting on November 3, a motion was approved that declared:

Whereas the Pacifist views expressed recently by our pastor . . . at the Southern Baptist Convention at New Orleans and the expression of views of a similar nature, both in private to the members of the congregation, and in the pulpit of our church, have in the opinion of the Board of Deacons, greatly weakened his influence, now therefore be it resolved that . . . he tender his resignation to the church, believing that by so doing he will save both himself and the church further embarrassment and will strengthen the work of the church in this community.

Taylor responded to the deacons two days later:

The disquieting affairs of the First Baptist Church were submitted to a full meeting of the official Board of the church July 8th last, with the assurance that I would cheerfully conform to any course the brethren might agree upon. Since then the whole question has been in the Board's hands. Many individuals have expressed their opinions pro and con, and many rumors have been afloat. Only recently has the Board reached an agreement and it is the first authoritative statement that has been made. This preamble states my position fairly and fraternally. I am a pacifist both for church and state. I regret that what seems to be my best interests in a secular way does not meet my convictions of duty in this case. But I in no wise admit that a pacifist is not a patriot. As our country is in war, I am absolutely loyal to the country's interest in every fibre of my being; and I am confident that the pacifist will be more popular later than he is today.

Taylor was forced to resign as pastor and retreated to Leaksville, North Carolina. Nevertheless, he resented being called a pacifist and sought vindication from the executive committee of the Southern Baptist Convention on allegations of disloyalty and lack of patriotism.

Things only got worse in American Christianity as the war continued. It was bad enough that in battle after senseless battle, Christian soldiers in World War I shot, bombed, torpedoed, burned, gassed, bayoneted, and starved each other and civilians until twenty million of them were wounded and another twenty million lay dead. But the actions of Christians at home in the United States during the Great war was shameful as well. Churches became willing servants of the state, contributing to wartime hysteria and propaganda. Clergymen in the pulpit and their followers in the pew both succumbed to war psychology and societal pressure just as most other citizens. One Baptist pastor said that he looked "upon the enlistment of an American solider" as he did "on the departure of a missionary for Burma." Not Taylor. During his time in North Carolina, he wrote a powerful book that was published in 1920, *The God of War*, that traces the folly of war from ancient times to World War I. I have never read such a radical treatise against war from the pen of a Christian minister.

In his foreword, Taylor explains that the views he sets forth "are the result of studies that have extended intermittently through thirty years, and of work similarly through four." He sends the volume forth "with the devout desire that it may confirm in the faith of the gospel the hearts of all who name the name of Christ, and that through their renewed fidelity to the truth it may hasten the day when the demon of hatred and deadly strife shall be driven from the whole world and men of all nations and tongues shall be brought into brotherhood and into peaceful and happy harmony with the will of God, as it is set forth in Jesus Christ." The book itself, in nine chapters and 255 pages, is a *tour de force*. A notice in a local newspaper, the *Clinch Valley News*, in April of 1922, said of the book:

A book written by Rev. Dr. J. J. Taylor, pastor of the First Baptist church of Leaksville, N. C., should have a wide circulation. To read Dr. Taylor['s] "God of War" is to have one's eyes opened to the folly, wickedness, infidelity and devilishness of wars. The first war was started and led by the devil, and he has been at it ever since, and will still do business at the old stand. Every nation under heaven is either prepared or preparing for war, else why navies and standing armies? A million people should read Dr. Taylor's book, and we sincerely believe the dawn of universal peace would be hastened.

In "Among the Gods," Taylor points out how the ancients all had a war god in their pantheon of gods. The brutal Teutonic conception of Valhalla, where the war god awaited his faithful servants, was at least consistent, "Certainly it did not present the absurdity which some preachers have lately proclaimed, that men who hate and kill one another in battle are welcomed to the Better Land, where they forget the animosities which they have cherished and the wounds and deaths which they have inflicted, and together praising the Prince of Peace." In Rome the war god was called Mars. But not only did the war god eventually assume the supreme place in the pantheon, "in some important respects he has kept it to this day." Indeed, "history records no case in which warring peoples have failed to call upon the god of battles for his blessing on their bloody deeds." Taylor notes that during the Great War some American ministers "proceeded to preach and to pray in terms quite as provincial and profane as anything heard in England or Germany." But in all these utterances, "none of them mention the name of Jesus, who forbids violence and commands non-resistance and love."

Instead, they "all alike appeal to a provincial god, who in each case is supposed to favour one class of his creatures in their fell desire to hurt and to kill and to destroy others of the same blood and so to fill the world with additional bereavement and woe." And furthermore, "each assumes that such a god will side with him and against those whom he wishes to destroy, or even to send to hell."

In "The War God Honoured," Taylor explains how the war god is honored "in the honours accorded his servants." In Homer's day, as now, "men distinguished in battle became the people's idols." Taylor points out that "men distinguished with the title Great have invariably been men of blood, who ruthlessly crushed out the lives of their fellow-men." Men known in history as Alexander, Constantine, Charles, Peter, and Frederick the Great, and those less conspicuous like Xerxes, Attila, and Napoleon, were "high priests in the service of the god of carnage and destruction." In one of the few quotes in *The God of War* from other writers, Taylor sounds like he is describing the year 2015: "Public sentiment is so perverted that military service is regarded as the all-sufficient qualification for any office or position; and no rewards, pecuniary, professional, civil, are adequate compensation for having been connected directly or remotely, usefully or as a drone, with an army." Taylor relates how "all the forms of literature glorify the war god in glorifying his servants." And "the public press is true to form, when it announces the names of those killed in the effort to kill others as Our Heroes." "History," concludes Taylor, "is largely a story of the wars which states and nations have waged."

In "The War God a Saviour," Taylor mentions the cliché we still hear today about a boy joining the military and coming out "a manlier man" who is more self-reliant and courageous. This, of course, on the assumption that he comes out, "otherwise the helpless parent can think about how much more precious the soil is made by the dead boy's blood." "The war god's supreme glory," declares Taylor, "is found in being a saviour of souls." Taylor asserts that the Muslim idea that every man killed in battle "secures the favour of Allah and an abundant entrance into his presence" is likewise held in Germany, England, France, Belgium, Canada, and America where "the idea widely prevails that the service of the war god saves." Those who die in battle are ushered into God's presence as his faithful servants. But, as Taylor explains, "If such service was sufficient to save them and take them home to glory, there is no place for the doctrine of atonement through the blood of Christ."

In "The War God's Pleas," Taylor relates how the war god "usually inspires his servants with some sort of excuse for any particular war which he leads them to undertake." Conquest, revenge, liberty, patriotism, religion, slavery, and peace—all are used by the war god in his pleas for war. Taylor marvels that "under the domination of the war god the man who loves his country too well to want her plunged into the maelstrom of war is not considered a patriot." And it is not just the religion of paganism that is used by the war god. "Various corrupted forms of Christianity" have also been used "to kindle strife and spill blood." But Christians who serve the war god and have "resorted to carnal weapons and physical force in a vain effort to dethrone evil and establish righteousness in the earth" have forgotten that "spiritual weapons under the power of God are mighty enough to overthrow every stronghold of Satan and bring complete conquest." The war god so warps the minds of men that "they trample the law under foot, and go forth hating men and working desolation and death, and are yet able to look the world in the face and say they are doing their dreadful work in the interest of life and peace."

In "Temples and Sacrifices," Taylor points out that "from times remote the god of war has instigated the erection of massive and ornate temples in his honour." Just imagine what Taylor would say about the Pentagon. But even in nations that have not erected such structures, "they have conceived and establish institutions for the avowed purpose of diverting young men from the paths of peace, filling them with the spirit of class and caste, obliterating the idea of equality and brotherhood, teaching them to dominate their fellow-men and to lead them out to waste their lives in camps and barracks or perchance to destroy themselves in the effort to destroy others." Taylor avows that "the god of war has no concern for the welfare of his subjects.," and that "his demands extend to every form of material wealth and every treasure of sacred sentiment." But because these demands are "insatiable," the sacrifices in the end "represent absolute and irreparable waste." Throughout history, "desolation followed every army, whether in victory or defeat." The "herding of men together in the service of the war god inevitably produces filth and foulness and all the conditions that induce pestilence." Taylor laments that "in modern times the genius of man has been taxed to the utmost to invent more effective means of destruction, and these are cited as evidences of advancing civilization." Taylor calls World War I a "crime." He denounced the draft. He condemns the Espionage Act and the prohibitions on freedom of speech and of the press that were enacted by the United States during the war. He criticizes chaplains who profess to believe in the "doctrine of separation between church and state" but "ask and accept commissions to preach under government control and for government pay." He chastises Christian bodies that "formally commit themselves to the work of wounding and killing their enemies by all the devices of modern warfare." Mothers love the service of Molech more than they love their sons when they glory in sending them off to war.

In "The War God Identified," Taylor relates how the war god is a god of lust. He sees a connection between war lust and sex lust. The early conquerors "rose to power, and forthwith established harems." Down through history, "armies have been full of filth." Venereal diseases "have always been in the armies of nations the dominant cause of disability." Taylor agrees with another writer who says: "Wherever there are troops, especially in war time, there are bad women and weak women, and the result is inevitable: a certain number of both officers and men go astray." The attitude of soldiers toward women is "immodest, unmoral, objective, evaluating and experimental." Taylor also charges the war god with being a god of cruelty and crime who "has gripped the minds of the best educated people on the globe, and driven them to do his barbarous work."

In "God and the War God" Taylor points out how "the servants of the war god make a general appeal to the Bible, especially the Old Testament, in justification of what they call their glorious work." But, explains Taylor, "the mere fact that the Bible says much about wars and rumours of wars in no wise indicates God's approval; nor does the record of wars waged by good men, such as Abraham or Moses, Joshua or Caleb, justify the conclusion that God approves

of wars waged by men whom he has not authorized to make war."
Taylor criticizes the practice by "savage militarists and devotees of
the war god" of appealing to the nuances of Hebrew words in the
Old Testament in their attempt to limit the meaning of the commandment "Thou shalt not kill" to murder, as if war is not murder
on a grand scale. Nothing has changed. This is exactly what modern evangelical warvangelicals do. Modern war lords "presume or
play the hypocrite when they claim that God has sent them to kill
thousands." Taylor points out, as I have done many times, that "God
never commissioned any other nation or people to make war" other
than Old Testament Israel.

In "Jesus and the War God," Taylor argues that Jesus "es-
chewed the methods of the war god" and did not at any time resort
"to violence to enforce his will." Indeed, Jesus "chose to die rather
than resort to violence and the shedding of human blood." Taylor recounts how the second-century Greek philosopher Celsus
"fiercely assailed Christianity for its adherents' "lack of patriotism"
and refusal "to take up arms and kill men over political questions."
He mentions the pacifism of the early church and the Church Fathers. Christian militarists have against them "not only the teachings of the Scriptures, but also the protest of eminent Christian
men through the centuries." Christian militarists "are renouncing
their own moral principles" and betraying their Lord when they
"voluntarily give themselves up to the foul work of war and will-
ingly partake of its cruelties and crimes by offering their means to
make it effective." Taylor mocks Christian militarists who believe
that although the "entire spirit of the New Testament is the spirit of
peace," they are not yet ready to quit and follow Christ. Referring to
the men in Luke chapter nine who said they would follow the Lord
but only after they buried their dead and bid farewell to their family,
Taylor has Christian militarists say to the Lord: "Lord, I will follow
thee; but let me first go and stifle my wicked enemies with poisoned
gas and smash them with exploding shells and wreck them with
machine guns and send them to hell, so the world may be safe for
democracy."

In "The War God Repudiated?," Taylor goes after the "money
grubbers, who rush for government contracts" and "are ready for

the thousands to be ground in the war god's cruel mill, if thereby they can pile up larger wealth." He points out how nations, "however averse to war on the part of others," claim for themselves "the right to wage war" and in every case judge their wars "to be just and righteous." And like the nations, "the churches also stand for war." Taylor mentions the submission and rejection of his peace resolution at the 1917 meeting of the Southern Baptist Convention and how he was "hooted and hissed and threatened with personal violence by honourable members of the body." He laments that "not a single great religious body made any protest against the crimes of war, or expressed any regret for the desolation and misery it caused." To the contrary, "Many of them warmly endorsed it and pledged it their hearty support." During World War I, to the shame of Christianity, "Thoughtful men outside the Church, Agnostics, Jews, unbelievers of various schools, quietly noted the failure of Christianity, and were confirmed in their unbelief." Combatants in the Great War, with their "thin veneer of Christianity," "conformed more to Mohammed's teaching rather than to Christ's." They fought with fury equal to their pagan allies as they went forth "to establish righteousness and peace by violence and blood." In America, where the Church "boasted of its freedom from state control," it participated voluntarily, leaving Jesus "out of its war councils," and rendering "unto Caesar the things it had dedicated unto God."

I am pleased to report that Taylor was vindicated. He apparently did not attend the meeting of the Southern Baptist Convention in Hot Springs, Arkansas, in 1918. But after attending the annual meeting in 1919, 1920, and 1921, Taylor was elected vice-president of the Southern Baptist Convention at its meeting in Jacksonville, Florida, in 1922. He was nominated by J. W. Porter, who had clashed with him at the 1917 meeting. A report by the Commission on Social Service praised the participation of the United States in a conference on disarmament.

At the 1923 meeting of the Southern Baptist Convention in Kansas City, Missouri, Taylor offered, and the Convention adopted, a resolution which described war as "one of the most ghastly and grievous burdens that afflict the human family" and resolved that members of the Convention who attended the upcoming meeting of the Baptist World Alliance urge that group to "make a clear and concise deliverance on War, which shall be in full harmony with the spirit and teachings of our Lord Christ, as set forth in the Holy Scriptures."

At the 1924 meeting of the Southern Baptist Convention in Atlanta, Georgia, Taylor moved that a Peace Committee be appointed to "prepare and present at the next annual meeting of this body, a paper setting forth the Christian teaching with reference to war." Seven men were appointed, including Taylor. The Committee on Resolutions recommended that two anti-war resolutions be referred to this Peace Committee. Because the newly adopted 1925 Baptist Faith and Message included a three-paragraph section on "Peace and War" at the instigation of the Peace Committee, the Peace Committee felt it "unnecessary to make further recommendation" to the Convention.

The three paragraphs read as follows:

> XIX. Peace and War
>
> It is the duty of Christians to seek peace with all men on principles of righteousness. In accordance with the spirit and teachings of Christ they should do all in their power to put an end to war.
>
> The true remedy for the war spirit is the pure gospel of our Lord. The supreme need of the world is the acceptance of his teachings in all the affairs of men and nations, and the practical application of his law of love.
>
> We urge Christian people throughout the world to pray for the reign of the Prince of Peace, and to oppose everything likely to provoke war.

I am not pleased to report that this last statement was removed beginning with the 1963 edition of the Baptist Faith and Message. If you want to know what happened to the Southern Baptists see my article "What Happened to the Southern Baptists?"

Taylor died in January of 1930. His memory has been kept alive by Bill Sumners of the Southern Baptist Historical Library and Archives, whom I am greatly indebted to for some material on Taylor and for his own writings on Taylor. For my part, I have reprinted Taylor's *The God of War* as part of my Classic Reprints series.

Joseph Judson Taylor is what all Baptist ministers should have been during World War I. He is what all Baptist ministers should be today. He is what all ministers of any denomination should have been and should be. Although Taylor and his pacifism have been long forgotten, they are an antidote to the militaristic climate that exists throughout Christendom today.[1]

---

1. https://www.lewrockwell.com/2015/03/laurence-m-vance/man-of-peace/

EXHIBIT F

J. J. Taylor Essay by Bill Sumners

and used with his permission

JOSEPH JUDSON TAYLOR, PACIFIST AND ANTI-EVOLUTIONIST: BIBLICAL LITERALISM AT ITS BEST

M. P. Hunt, special correspondent for the Baptist World, published out of Louisville, gave this report of the Saturday evening session of the 1917 Southern Baptist Convention meeting in New Orleans.

Dr. J. J. Taylor of Savannah, GA., in speaking to the report, brought on a scene indescribable. He thought the convention had too much of Caesar and too little of God. Hate, hate, he charged as characterizing the public mind today. He deplored the gloating and hand clapping over human beings being shot to death. War, he held, was un-Christian and if we enter it, humility and not gloating should mark our decorum.

When Taylor was challenged by messengers from the floor, "Some cried treason and while his remarks squinted in that direction, yet the charge was unfortunate. In all of our twenty-five years in the Convention we have never seen it so wrought up. Judging from the smile upon his face (Taylor) our brother actually gloried in the raging tempest he had created. One of his worst thrusts was the implication that most everybody but himself was worshiping a provincial God. The Teuton God he held was cordially hated. When at last Taylor yielded the floor, Dr. Truett poured oil on the troubled waters. As he lifted us in prayer to a throne of grace, the Convention came back to itself."[1]

Who was J. J. Taylor and what had gotten the Convention so wrought up? Joseph Judson Taylor was born November 1, 1855 in Henry County, Virginia. He graduated with a masters degree from Richmond College in 1881. Upon awarding the only Master's diploma that year the College Faculty Chair quoted from Aesop's fable, "Unum sed leonem" "One –but he is a lion."[2]

J. M. L. Curry advised Taylor to attend the Newton Theological Seminary, but Taylor preferred Southern associations. He enrolled in the Baptist seminary in Louisville and attended classes, but never graduated from Southern Seminary. Later, Taylor received honorary doctorates from Howard College (Samford) and Union University. During his ministry, he served as pastor to significant churches in Georgia, Alabama, Tennessee, and Kentucky. On two occasions he was elected Vice-President of the Southern Baptist Convention, and he also gave the Convention sermon in 1899. He authored at least five books and often expressed himself in Baptist newspapers in the form of articles and letters.

Taylor was basically a biblical literalist. He attacked Harry Fosdick for doubting the certainty of the Virgin Birth. "In repudiating the Virgin Birth Dr. Fosdick necessarily repudiates the inerrancy of Scriptures," Taylor wrote in the *Western Recorder*. Taylor took on the role of speaking for the Baptist common man and accused Biblical liberals of making the Bible "a book replete with fables and falsehoods."[3]

His biggest targets related to biblical literalism were evolution and modernism. He was openly critical of Baptists who identified themselves as theistic evolutionist. Again in the pages of the *Western Recorder*, he blasted Wake Forest College president William L.

1. *Baptist World*, May 31, 1917, p. 7–8.
2. *Baptist Biography*, v. 3, p. 430.
3. *Western Recorder*, October 5, 1922.

Poteat for accepting and teaching theistic evolution. Taylor concluded, "If these things are taught at Wake Forest College, the institution is quite in line with the rationalistic schools of Germany and France, and there is no reason whatever why any Baptist should put another dollar into it."[4] Taylor was sympathetic to J. Frank Norris' battle against evolutionists but questioned Norris' violent behavior which resulted in him being charged with murder. Taylor hoped that "he would come out of the fearful experience chastened and prepared to do his work in a less violent spirit."[5] Taylor finalized his attacks on Darwin with his book entitled *Evolution Theory: Plain words for plain folks.*[6]

For a biblical literalist to be an anti-evolutionist is no surprise. But Taylor's belief in an inerrant Bible also led him to some surprising conclusions. For him, Scripture was completely reliable in all areas of life. In a letter debate in the *Alabama Baptist* Taylor made his strong arguments against capital punishment. He responded to an article by evangelist A.V. Reese, who according to Taylor, pleaded "for the ancient custom of killing criminals." Reese himself was replying to an article by *Alabama Baptist* editor, L.L. Gwaltney who questioned the morality of the death penalty. Taylor raised nine questions that cast doubt on the legalized killing by the state. Among them he asked, "If the Alabama legislature can annul the authority of the sixth commandment for the state's official butcher, why can it not annul the authority of the other nine?" He also reasoned, "How can a Christian man who devoutly prays for the salvation of the lost, consistently approve killing a helpless sinner and hurrying him on to hell?" Taylor concluded with a challenge for proponents of capital punishment, "If Brother Reese or any other champions of human butchery can make satisfactory answers he will shed welcome light on a vital theme."[7]

---

4. *Western Recorder,* May 11, 1922, p. 5.

5. J.J. Taylor to J.E. Dillard, July 30, 1926. Joseph Judson Taylor Collection, SBHLA.

6. Taylor, Joseph Judson. *Evolution theory: plain words for plain folks.* Kansas City, Mo.: Publishers Press, 1926.

7. *Alabama Baptist,* March 5, 1926, p. 6.

Taylor, though, was to be ever-remembered by his colleagues for the events at the 1917 Southern Baptist Convention in the Crescent City. In April 1917, America entered the world war to make the world safe for democracy. The Southern Baptist Convention met in May and on the first day of the meeting, J. W. Porter, the fiery editor of the *Western Recorder*, proposed a resolution pledging Southern Baptist support to the President and the war effort. When Taylor tried to redirect the resolution, Porter shouted that he "could not conceive of men from the land of Lee and Jackson being opposed to such a resolution." The Convention messengers applauded Porter's remarks, voted down Taylor's motion, and passed the resolution. But Taylor was not finished. On the third day of the Convention, he presented his own series of peace resolutions. They read:

> Resolved: 1. That we deeply deplore the awful and sorrowful calamity which has caused these leading nations to drench the earth in the blood of their own loyal citizens.

> 2. That we affirm our faith in the righteousness of the Sermon on the Mount, and our confidence in the infallible wisdom of Him who taught us to love our enemies, to bless them that curse us, and to do good to them that despitefully use and persecute us.

> 3. That we desire a stronger faith in the God who maketh wars to cease even unto the ends of the earth, and we shall rejoice if our own people, and all of every name who love the Lord Jesus Christ in sincerity, shall find it in their hearts to pray for kings and all that are in authority, that we may live quiet and peaceable lives in all godliness and honesty.[8]

Many of the messengers interpreted the last resolve to imply praying for the Kaiser. The resolution failed, receiving only 112 votes.

On Saturday the convention heard a report from the Committee on the World Crisis. This committee included three significant leaders in Baptist life, R.H. Pitt, renowned editor of the *Religious Herald*, J. B. Gambrell, who had just been elected President of the

---

8. Southern Baptist Convention Annual, 1917, p. 74–75.

SBC and executive secretary of the Baptist General Convention of Texas, and E.Y. Mullins, President of Southern Seminary and probably the most widely known and respected Southern Baptist leader. The report, while deploring war, pledged Baptist support for the military effort. The report read:

Deeply as we all deplore war, ardently as we longed and labored to avert or avoid it, we may be cheered and heartened in remembering that we are moved in entering it neither by lust nor hate, but by the love of humanity.[9]

Taylor rose to oppose the report. Certainly many in the meeting had a clear sense of Taylor's feeling on the matter based on prior events at the Convention. He thought that such a resolution was out of keeping with the allowed purposes of the Convention and especially contrary to the teaching of Christ. He thought the Convention had rendered too many things to Caesar. He asked how America would meet God when she had been making millions out of the sale of war munitions. He wondered if some poor wretch who had been sent to hell by American powder would look up and call for Mr. Dupont to dip his finger in water to cool his tongue. War, he held, was unchristian, and if we enter it, "humility, not gloating should mark our decorum." Some messengers in the Convention shouted treason and tried to have him ruled out of order. J.W. McCall of Kentucky raised a point of personal privilege, and asked "Is there no way to protect ourselves as loyal Americans from the treasonable utterances of this man?" One witness wrote that Taylor was the "center of the stormiest scene that was ever enacted on the floor of the Convention." Taylor remembered that he was "hooted and hissed and threatened with personal violence by honorable members of the body." Taylor cast the only negative vote on the adoption of the report.[10]

The fallout of these events was considerable. Taylor went on a brief campaign to defend his actions at the New Orleans Convention. Taylor argued that his address at the convention with the presentation of his peace resolutions was carefully prepared and did "not

9. Southern Baptist Convention, *Annual,* 1917, p. 101.

10. Sumners, Bill. "Joseph Judson Taylor: A Baptist Pacifist. *Baptist Peacemaker; Baptist World*, May 31, 1917, p. 7–8; Christian Index, May 24, 1917, p. 22–23.

contain one single treasonable or disloyal utterance."[11] He claimed that he was in his rights as a member of the Convention to challenge certain actions by the assembly but was not the cause of the great disorder. Taylor voiced his confidence in the plain Baptists who did not attend "big, unruly Conventions" to judge for themselves who was right on this disagreeable matter.[12] In a letter to E. Y. Mullins in August, he stated his objection to "the church to which I belong taking formal part in this orgy of butchery and blood." Taylor, poking fun at SBC leaders wrote, "I am certainly glad that the government assumes the entire responsibility, and relieves my brethren of any denominational responsibility in the desolating work of war."[13] As late as December of 1917, Taylor continued to seek vindication of himself against charges of disloyalty. He petitioned the newly formed Executive Committee of the Southern Baptist Convention to consider the incident at the New Orleans Convention and asked them to "exonerate him of all allegations of disloyalty and lack of patriotism." Taylor maintained that he had not been given a square deal or a fair hearing before the church body.[14]

Taylor did have his defenders. A. J. Dickinson, pastor of the First Baptist Church of Birmingham, defended Taylor's actions in a letter to the *Baptist World*. He believed that the "Saturday night clash" grew out of an intolerance of some of the "belligerent brethren in the Convention toward Dr. Taylor's pronounced pacifism." Dickinson regretted that such an important issue did not receive more adequate consideration and discussion in a more mature manner. He believed the "war-mania of the belligerent brethren would not suffer the Convention to consider the militant pacifism of Dr. Taylor's resolutions; and so the Convention is left, though unwarrantably so, in the light of having repudiated the Word of God on this matter from Genesis to Revelation." The Birmingham pastor concluded his defense of Taylor by declaring that if this war is won for the establishment of peace and social justice, it is going

11. *Religious Herald*, June 7, 1917, p. 6.

12. *Religious Herald*, June 14, 1917, p. 14.

13. J. J. Taylor to E. Y. Mullins, August 20, 1917, Joseph Judson Taylor Collection. SBHLA.

14. *Atlanta Constitution*, December 20, 1917, p. 9.

to be done, not by those who are "on a war-drunk but by the militant pacifist, willing to purchase peace for the earth at the price of war. . .."[15]

Taylor returned to his pastorate at the First Baptist Church of Savannah, Georgia, and preached a sermon entitled, "The Divided Kingdom." In this sermon, Taylor, explained that the faith community is "not called to usurp the place of Congress in declaring war, nor is it appointed to gather arms or even to sell bonds to put money into the national treasury." The church is set apart from the state to offer a prophetic voice concerning justice, mercy, humility and the right relationship with God. It could not afford to give formal sanction to the shedding of human blood.[16]

This and the episode at the SBC did not go well with some of the membership of the First Baptist Church of Savannah. In November, the Deacons of the Baptist Church at Savannah noted that "the Pacifist views expressed recently by our pastor . . . at the Southern Baptist Convention in New Orleans and the expression of views of a similar nature, both in private to the members of the congregation, and in the pulpit of our church, have in the opinion of the Board of Deacons, greatly weakened his influence" and called for his resignation. Taylor gave a generous response to the deacons and the church, declaring his absolute loyalty to his country's interest, but noted "I am confident that the pacifist will be more popular later than he is today."[17] A decade later, B.J.W. Graham, Baptist editor and biographer, wrote "at this time they [resolutions] would probably pass the same body without a dissenting voice, so clearly is the correctness of Dr. Taylor's position recognized." The *Baptist Witness* wrote, "Perhaps the denomination never made a greater blunder, and was never more criticized for any action it had taken.[18]

Taylor retreated to his home county of Leaksville, North Carolina and served a church in that community, but was relatively

---

15. *Atlanta Constitution*, December 20, 1917, p. 9.

16. Parham, Robert, *Light*, July/August, 1986, p. 5; Christian Index, July 5, 1917, p. 7.

17. Baptist Church at Savannah, Georgia, Minutes, November 5, 1917.

18. Graham, B.J. W. *Baptist Biography*, vol. 3, p. [page number missing in original essay. JL].

silent on war and peace issues. In 1920, he continued his pacifist crusade in his book, *The God of War*. This lengthy work traces war from ancient times to World War I. In his preface he stated that the purpose of the book was to hasten the day when the "demon of hatred and deadly strife shall be driven from the world and men of all nations and tongues shall be brought unto brotherhood and unto peaceful and happy harmony with the will of God, as it is set forth in Jesus Christ." Greed, on part of the munitions makers, had pushed America to war, Taylor wrote. But the masses of Christians would be true of heart, Taylor predicted. This remnant would not have Christ return and find their hands red in the blood of their enemies. These faithful pacifists will teach every man that the Lord speaks peace to all nations and extends his dominion over all the world. This, Taylor believed, is the way to destroy the war god.

Taylor apparently recovered somewhat from the episode at the 1917 Convention. In 1922 he became pastor of the First Baptist Church in Jasper, Alabama, serving there until 1927. In 1922, he was elected vice-president of the Convention, defeating J. W. Porter, who had clashed with him at the 1917 meeting. At the 1923 SBC, he succeeded in getting the convention to pass a resolution condemning war and urging the Baptist World Alliance to "make a clear concise deliverance on war . . . as set forth in the Holy Scriptures."[19]

At the 1924 SBC, Taylor made a motion that a peace committee be established to report to the 1925 session on the Bible and peace. His motion passed. Taylor was one of the seven appointed to this committee. In the intervening year, the peace committee asked the Committee on the Baptist Faith and Message Statement to include a section on peace in its report. At the 1925 SBC meeting, the peace committee said it found the paragraph in the Baptist Faith and Message statement acceptable and, therefore, the convention did not have to hear its recommendations. The pacifist Taylor had finally succeeded in getting the SBC to make a strong statement on peace.[20]

19. Parham, *Light*, July/August, 1986 p. 6; Southern Baptist Convention, *Annual*, 1923, p. 46.

20. Parham, *Light*, July/August, 1986, p. 6.

The pacifism of Joseph Judson Taylor came from his belief in an inerrant Bible that centered on the teachings and actions of Jesus. This belief called for the rejection of violence and the commandment to love your enemies. Baptist fundamentalists are not necessarily warmongers. The truth is that a literal interpretation of scripture can lead to pacifism. This Baptist minister's pacifism was enhanced by the strong doctrine of a "complete separation between church and state."[21] Each has a particular sphere of influence and obligation, but one did not trump the other –in particular, state action did not supplant matters of faith. The "Peace and War" sections of all three Baptist Faith and Message Statements, which are essentially the same, have roots in Baptist pacifism. The dogged determination of J. J. Taylor makes this a noteworthy element of our Baptist heritage.

21. *Christian Index*, July 5, 1917, p. 7.

EXHIBIT G

A Dietrich Recall

I REPENT, I RECANT, AND I APOLOGIZE TO THE GHOST OF DIETRICH BONHOEFFER

In the spirit of Detroit's recall of defective automobiles, I would like to issue a recall of criticism that for many years I have uncritically but understandably heaped upon the head of Dietrich Bonhoeffer for what now appears to me to be a defective charge against him for complicity in plots to assassinate Adolph Hitler. In short, in spite of a popular and common view about his complicity and in spite of my diligent search for such, I have not seen one shred of evidence implicating him in any such plots. Accordingly, in the marvelous spirit of Sam Houston who once even apologized to his horse for cursing at it, I withdraw anything I have ever said or written that implies such complicity. Note carefully, however, that I am not asserting that Bonhoeffer was not complicit in any way. Negatives are still very hard to prove. I am only stating that I have not seen a shred of evidence that he was; and in the process I have seen much evidence to suggest he was not. This first paragraph constitutes the totality of my repentance, recall, and apology. All that follows is simply background for how this came about and is not required reading. But it is to help keep you from falling into the same avoidable trap.

Fortunately I am such an unknown quantity that I don't need to take out a front-page advertisement in the *New York Times* to rectify what I have said, as only a handful of people have ever read or heard my volcanic eruptions over the topic. Fortunately, one of those readers who himself seemed inclined to the same view as mine about Bonhoeffer's guilt, asked me one day during a robust but nevertheless fraternal exchange what evidence I had for my view. The only immediate answer I had to that question was what I have read and heard at the popular level that included a biography of Bonhoeffer by the celebrated Eric Metaxas. Metaxas, whose book assumes and perpetuates the view I have come to abandon, symbolizes at the ostensible scholarly level the masses who have come to accept Bonhoeffer's complicity. I am no longer among those masses.

The reason I have abandoned the complicity paradigm is rooted initially in the challenge of my friend for evidence. Finding none on the Wikipedia entry for Bonhoeffer, an entry that simply asserts Bonhoeffer was accused of complicity but provides not a shred of court testimony to substantiate the charge, I did what I usually do in such circumstances: I turned to my scholarly friends. To about forty of them, I sent the following statement in an email:

> Dear fellow historians and friends who might be interested,
>
> A dear friend of mine has challenged my understanding of Bonhoeffer's guilt in connection with the plot to assassinate Hitler. I freely grant his challenge, as I have simply uncritically adopted the popular view. He might very well be right. While I have no dog in the fight, I would still like to be right. But maybe I need to repent. Any help you might provide in resolving this question would be appreciated. As friends I hope you will consider immediately dropping whatever you are doing right now and address my parochial concern.
>
> Very truly yours,
>
> JL

To this email I received the following reply from my dear friend, William Kostlevy, a Notre Dame PhD in history and the Director of the Brethren Historical Library and Archives in Elgin, Illinois:

Jim,

You might want to check out the book by Mark Thiessen Nation, Anthony Siegrist, and Daniel Umbel, *Bonhoeffer: The Assassin?* I haven't looked at in a few years; but as I remember they suggest that Bonhoeffer, while active in the Abwehr resistance (in part, by the way, to avoid being drafted), was not necessarily involved in the actual murder plot. One issue is that Eberhard Bethge, Bonhoeffer's friend and major biographer, was critical of Bonhoeffer's views as expressed in *Cost of Discipleship*. As you can tell I have dropped what I am doing to sort of answer your question but I suspect a real friend would have re-read *Bonhoeffer the Assassin?* and given you a definitive answer.

William Kostlevy
Director Brethren Historical Library and Archives
1451 Dundee Ave.
Elgin, IL 60120
847-742-5100 ext 368

Upon receiving the gift of this reply, I immediately went to ebay and found a copy of Mark Nation's book for $5.00, down from the original price of $29.99. I waited for it anxiously every day; and when it finally did arrive, I dropped everything myself and immediately read chapter three, entitled "Dietrich Bonhoeffer, the Assassin?" That chapter by itself satisfactorily answered my question about the existence of any evidence for Bonhoeffer's complicity. The short answer: none.

With this information in hand, I found the author's email address online (mark.nation@emu.edu) and sent him this memo:

Dear Mark Nation,

Your co-authored book just arrived in today's mail. I only came across it recently. Dr. William Kostlevy of the Brethren Archives in Chicago told me about it in response to an inquiry I sent out to maybe 40 friends, asking if any of them knew of a single shred of evidence that Bonhoeffer was complicit in the assassination plots. I had been encouraged to explore this subject by a former U.S. Ambassador with whom I was carrying on a robust but friendly exchange about the subject. It was his quite reasonable request for evidence that set me off down this trail. I was, like Stanley Hauerwas and seemingly even Eric Metaxas, an uncritical believer in the guilt of DB. Faced with his question, I immediately set off down that trail, turning beet-red at the embarrassing possibility that I had taken something at face value that I had no right to do, as it is my custom volcanically to pour literary lava on the frontal lobes of others who simply take things at face value. Painfully yanking several splinters, nails, and razor blades out of both of my own eyes, I found your book on ebay and bought it pronto. In short, I will be preparing a public recantation that I hope to circulate as widely as I have my assassination of DB's ghost. Fortunately I am so little known that I won't have much work to do. But the amount matters not. And in the process I hope to advertise your fine work. I was disappointed in it initially because I was hoping in one minute to see a sentence in your first paragraph that read "There is not a shred of evidence for DB's complicity." But ultimately I found it and you have made a convert out of me. I would not say that DB was not involved, as we cannot now know that. But I am comfortable asserting that any evidence for it has not yet surfaced and probably never will. If I err in any way in this calculation, please advise and spare me any further embarrassment. I have about used up my life's allotment.

In the event I have difficulty finding the email addresses of your co-authors, might I prevail upon you to forward this memo to them?

Fraternally yours for Christ and His Kingdom,

James Lutzweiler
Archivist (1999–2013), Southeastern Baptist Theological Seminary

EXHIBIT H

Meredith Willson's
Sunday School Class

An Abstract about Mason City's Music Man, Meredith Willson

From a Chapter Entitled

"A Biographical Dictionary of
My Friends, Family, and Familiar Faces"

In *The Autobiography of a Nobody*—which is more
euphemistically entitled *My First Five Thousand Lives:*

The Adventures of an Archivist and the Tunes of a Troubadour

BY JAMES LUTZWEILER

A Picture of the author in a former life or the next one, he isn't sure which

I never met Meredith Willson. I wish I had. But years ago I did get a letter from his widow in response to a question I sent her about the evangelist Billy Sunday and the composer of *76 Trombones in the Big Parade*—to say nothing of *May the Good Lord Bless and Keep You*, *It's Beginning to Look a Lot Like Christmas*, and *Till There Was You*, the lattermost of which the Beatles recorded. I was more interested in Willson's possible connection to Billy and the Bible than to the Beatles.

The connection I thought might be there, but wasn't, involved trombones. Billy Sunday, also born in Iowa, had conducted a revival in Willson's Mason City, Iowa, in June 1904. At that time Willson had just celebrated his second birthday (May 18, 1902) but I did not know that yet. While it is quite possible and even probable that Willson's mother and Methodist Sunday school teacher had taken him with her to Sunday's revival meetings, it is doubtful the lad would have remembered anything from them anyway. What I did know was that Billy Sunday's famous songleader (and also a Methodist), Homer Rodeheaver, was a celebrated trombonist; and I had simply begun to wonder if perhaps Willson's play, *The Music Man* with its 76 trombones, might have been rooted in Sunday's music maestro. It was not for more than one reason. Rodeheaver did not even join Sunday's evangelistic team until six years after Billy's Mason City exercises.

But I did not go away empty in my unsuccessful quest for a good story about Billy and Willy—if I might respectfully just nickname Willson here for mnemonic purposes. The story involved Willson and his mother. My Iowa story will not be made into a movie like *Field of Dreams*, but it still isn't bad. With the proper retelling and digesting of it at a dinner table, it has the potential of adding at least one full day to the life of anyone who belly laughs at it. I hope it has added to mine, as I lost a few minutes of my own because of a real estate deal I once made in Mason City with the American Crystal Sugar Company, a deal that I thought would be sweet but turned out to be as hard on my arteries as the concrete manufactured by the neighboring Lehigh Cement Company.

Because Willson's widow was unable to provide me with any certifiable connection with Rodeheaver even later in his life, though she could not rule it out either, I looked to see if Willson had written an autobiography. He had. It is entitled *And There I Stood with My Piccolo*. In it the Mason City impresario tells a story that made my unsuccessful Sunday/Rodeheaver/Willson quest worthwhile.

The story was about Meredith and his mother in the Sunday school class she taught at Mason City's Methodist church. I have paid my respects to that church by making a pilgrimage to its pews to capture the fun flavor of what transpired there. What happened there was that one Sunday morning the boy Meredith invited a friend to attend the class with him. Critical to this story is that Willson's young friend lisped—or should I say "lithped"?

The Sunday school lesson that day was about the Exodus and the crossing of the Red Sea by Moses and a couple gazillion Israelites. Meredith's mother asked the class what they thought was the first thing these Israelites did upon reaching dry land on the other side. Willson's guest raised his little hand. Willson's mother called on him. He replied, "They pithed." Picture little scholars' muffled snickers.

In his book Willson recounted how his mother took the lithper's answer in perfect stride and invited other children to respond until she got the answer she was looking for—which, quite incidentally, is also a "p" word: They "p"rayed. When the class was over, Meredith and his mother went into the auditorium for the morning service through which they both sat. After the service, they walked home with nothing unusual in their conversation. However, once inside their house and safe from any possible sighting of her by the lithper, Willson witnessed his mother collapsing on the couch in uncontrollable laughter.

Since that day, I have done the same thing many times but usually at a dining room table or even when I type it all out like right now again. And "pith" is even a good biblical word that God used. See, e.g., I Kings 14:10. But so far as I know, "pith" has never been used with reference to the Exodus. But the lithper was no doubt correct. Surely the Israelites did pith, and he spoke better than he knew. It is one of the rare cases where reading something into the Bible is right. Pith happens.

EXHIBIT I

A Sketch of Scoundrel and Scalawag C.I. Scofield

Cyrus Ingerson Scofield
(a/k/a "Charlie Ingerson," 1843–1921)

Synopsis: Taking not just a single page from King James but 1,353 of them, Cyrus Ingerson Scofield helped the Holy Spirit to create an even better Bible for his own parochial eschatological purposes.

Biography: C. I. Scofield was either a scholar or a scoundrel— or perhaps a pinch of both. Born near Detroit, Michigan, he was ostensibly born again in St. Louis, Missouri, during a revival conducted there in 1879 by America's premier premillenialist, Dwight L. Moody. "Ostensibly" is the governing word, as Scofield told at least two different conversion stories and possibly several more.[1] Those stories began to unravel a bit in 1899 after he conducted the funeral service for the famed evangelist, thereby becoming too well known to tell more than one. But perhaps one of them was true.

Disturbing questions about the reality of Scofield's sanctification and his eschatology, the latter also having two aspects, have arisen because of a pattern of demonstrable deceit that continued from his pre-conversion conviction for fraud until his final curtain fell not too far from Broadway's theaters in New York. Though a Yankee

1. Lutzweiler, Many Conversions, p. 6ff.

EXHIBIT I

by birth, Scofield initially fought for the Confederacy until he went AWOL from Tennessee and relocated to Missouri. That desertion did not keep him from telling his biographer, shortly before meeting his Maker, that he was an Antietam-decorated Rebel who served all four years in Jefferson Davis's dominions and that he was only ten miles from Appomattox (According to Google, St. Louis is technically 753 miles from Appomattox) when Lee surrendered to Grant.[2]

In 1873 that same Grant, now President, would appoint Scofield, by then a lawyer and somewhat newly wedded, as the District Attorney for the State of Kansas. Resigning shortly thereafter in political disgrace, he moved to St. Louis and practiced both law and lawlessness until he had to flee to Wisconsin where he lived under an assumed name, Charley Ingerson. Jailed there and then returned to a St. Louis slammer pending trial, Scofield soon began his pretribulational pilgrimage, later telling his biographer that his conversion took place in his law office where he was conducting a successful practice. Other accounts had him converting in jail or in a rescue mission.

Thereafter, still in St. Louis, Scofield came under the influence of a noted premillenialist Presbyterian pastor, James H. Brookes. Brookes was one of the first fathers of American fundamentalism, and Scofield followed right behind him eschatologically. Within three years of his conversion, Scofield—with pending divorce suppressed and suspended preaching license redressed—moved to Dallas, Texas, to pastor a church. It was there that he began to accumulate an even greater stock of pretribulational perspectives that by 1909 he would incorporate into the *Scofield Reference Bible*, published by Oxford University Press. And like Charles Gallaudet Trumbull, his Oxford authorized hagiographer, Scofield contributed to a series of essays called *The Fundamentals* that were published between 1910 and 1915. These essays became the intellectual backbone of the fundamentalist movement that later produced the eschatologically focused Billy Graham, Jerry Falwell, Hal Lindsey, and Tim LaHaye (of *Left Behind* fame). Those views became institutionalized in Dallas

---

2. These details of Scofield's life come from Trumbull, his authorized biographer; Canfield, his devastating critic; and Rushing.

Theological Seminary and Philadelphia School of the Bible (now Cairn University), both inspired by Scofield.

Heresy: By means of his widely sold *Reference Bible* and his peripatetic participation in prophetic Bible conferences all across America, Scofield popularized a pre-existing perspective that the Second Coming of Jesus would occur in two stages. Critics contend such hermeneutical gymnastics could proliferate Parousias almost indefinitely. To his somewhat dubious credit, however, while King James beheaded people who disagreed with him, Scofield only re-headed them off in a different direction.

In addition, Scofield popularized the view that someday Jews would return *en masse* to Palestine and once again become an independent political entity with a right to possess that land, notwithstanding the rights of its current occupants. This return to an ancient paradigm would be a sign of the Second Coming, but which of his two Second Comings he did not specify.

Application: That Scofield or any Christian may own two versions of events and two feet of clay—sometimes up to the navel, neck, or noggin—should come as no surprise. Perhaps Scofield's past political pal, Kansas Senator John James Ingalls, prophesied correctly when he, having heard of his old crony's conversion, said, "No man can doubt the efficacy of the scheme of Christian salvation with the record of Scofield in view."[3] The more important and sobering question is, "How high is my own clay?"

---

3. Lutzweiler, quoted in *Many Conversions*, p. 35, but originally published on p. 4 of the December 28, 1899, edition of *The Kansas City* Journal.

Bibliography

Blum, Ruthie. *To Hell in a Handbasket: Carter, Obama and the Arab Spring.* USA: RVP, 2012.

Bonhoeffer, Dietrich. *Letters and Papers from Prison.* New York: Macmillan, 1968.

Bradley, James. *The Imperial Cruise: A Secret History of Empire and War.* Boston: Little, Brown and Company, 2009.

Brothers, Thomas. *Louis Armstrong's New Orleans.* New York: W.W. Norton & Company, 2006.

Canfield, Joseph M. *The Incredible Scofield and His Book.* Ross House Books, 2005.

Carter, Jimmy. *The Hornet's Nest: A Novel of the Revolutionary War.* New York: Simon & Schuster, 2004.

Creekmore, Marion V. *A Moment of Crisis: Jimmy Carter, The Power of a Peacemaker, and North Korea's Nuclear Ambitions* (New York: Public Affairs, 2006).

Dixon, A.C., et al., Editors. *The Fundamentals.* Grand Rapids: Bake Books, 1970.

Djilas, Milovan. *Conversations with Stalin.* New York: Harcourt, Brace and World, 1962.

Harper, Keith. *Send the Light: Lottie* Moon. Macon: Macon: Mercer University Press, 2002.

Hinson, Glenn E. "Baptist Attitudes Toward War and Peace Since 1914," *Baptist History and Heritage,* Winter, 2004.

Hitler, Adolph. *Mein Kampf.* New York: Houghton Mifflin, 1971.

Hoopes, Roy. *When the Stars Went to War: Hollywood and World War II.* New York: Random House, 1994.

Horowitz, David. *Jimmy Carter's War Against the Jews.* Los Angeles: Freedom Press, 2007.

James, Marquis. *The Raven: A Biography of Sam Houston.* Austin: The University of Texas Press, 1988.

Bibliography

Jordan, Clarence. *The Cotton Patch Version of Matthew and John: Including the Gospel of Matthew. . .and the First Eight Chapters of the Gospel of John*. New York: Association Press, 1970.

Kahan, Stuart. *The Wolf of the Kremlin: The First Biography of L.M. Kaganovich, The Soviet Union's Architect of Fear*. William Morrow and Company, Inc. 1987.

Kanamaru, Eiko. "Japanese Baptists' compromise with nationalism in 1941," *Baptist History and Heritage*, Winter-Spring, 2001.

Link, Arthur S. *The Papers of Woodrow Wilson: Complete in 69 Volumes*. Princeton: Princeton University Press, 1966–1994.

Lutzweiler, David. *The Praise of Folly: The Enigmatic Life and Theology of C.I. Scofield*. No city cited: Apologetics Group Media, 2009.

Lutzweiler, James, Contributor. *Churchfails: One-Hundred Blunders in Church History (and What We Can Learn from Them)*. Nashville: B&H Publishing Group, 2016.

Lutzweiler, James, "Dietrich Bonhoeffer." Unpublished essay for *Churchfails*. Nashville: Broadman and Holman Publishing Group, 2016.

Lutzweiler, James. "Fundamentalism." Entry in *Encyclopedia of North Carolina*, edited by William S. Powell. Chapel Hill:The University of North Carolina Press, 2006.

Lutzweiler, James. "The Many Conversions of Fundamentalist Saint, Cyrus Ingerson Scofield: "Peer Among Scalawags" and the Golden Goose of Oxford University Press." A Pamphlet. Jamestown, NC: Schnappsburg University Press, 2009.

MacPherson, Dave. *The Great Rapture Hoax*. Fletcher, NC: Brand New Puritan Library, 1983.

Meigs, Mark. *Optimism at Armageddon: Voices of American Participants in the First World War*. NYC: New York University Press, 1997.

Milne, David. *America's Rasputin: Walt Rostow and the Vietnam War*. New York: Hill and Wang, 2008.

Nation, Mark Thiessen, et al. *Bonhoeffer the Assassin? Challenging the Myth, Recalling His Call to Peacemakng*. Grand Rapids: Baker Academic, 2013.

Owen, Robert L. *The Russian Imperial Conspiracy, 1892–1914: The Most Gigantic Intrigue of All Time* (New York: Albert and Charles Boni, 1927).

Parker, Calvin F. *The Southern Baptist Missionary Enterprise in Japan, 1889—1989*. Lanham, MD: University Press of America, 1990.

Payne, Robert. *Life and Death of Lenin*. New York: Simon & Schuster, 1964.

Priest, Gerald L. "William Jennnings Bryan and the Scopes Trial: A Fundamentalist Perspective." *Detroit Baptist Seminary Journal*, Volume 4, Fall 1999, 51–83. Also online at https://drive.google.com/file/d/1PzCQXJ3tLaboRIEGPedOxxLBn8GqEWVu/view.

Rushing, Jean. "From Confederate Deserter to Decorated Veteran Bible Scholar: Exploring the Enigmatic Life of C.I. Scofield, 1861–1921." M.A. thesis for East Tennessee State University, 2011.

Rusten, E. Michael. *A Critical Evaluation of Dispensational Interpretations of the Book of Revelation*. PhD dissertation for New York University, 1977.

Saunders, Francis W. "Love and Guilt: Woodrow Wilson and Mary Hulbert." *American Heritage*, April-May, 1979, volume 30, issue 3. Also online at https://www.americanheritage.com/love-and-guilt-woodrow-wilson-and-mary-hulbert.

Stabnow, David, ed. *Churchfails: 100 Blunders in Church History & What We Can Learn from Them*. Nashville: B&H Publishing Group, 2016.

Stassen, Glenn. "Harry Truman as Baptist President," *Baptist History and Heritage*, June, 1999.

Stinnett, Robert. *Day of Deceit: The Truth about FDR and Pearl Harbor*. Free Press, 1999.

Sumners, Bill. "Joseph Judson Taylor, Pacifist and Anti-evolutionist: Biblical Literalism at its Best." An unpublished paper read by author Sumners at the 2012 meeting of the Baptist History and Heritage Society in Raleigh, North Carolina.

Taylor, J. J. *The God of War*. No publishing details available but can be seen online at https://www.abebooks.com/servlet/BookDetailsPL?bi=30603928633&cm_sp=Searchmod-_-Nul lResults-_-BDP.

Tindall, George Brown and David E. Shi. *America: A Narrative History*. New York: W.W. Norton & Company, 2004.

Tolstoy, Leo. *The Kingdom of God is Within You*. Lincoln: University of Nebraska press, 1984.

Trumbull, Charles Gallaudet. *The Life Story of C. I. Scofield*. New York: Oxford University Press, 1920; and Eugene, Oregon: Wipf & Stock Publishers, 2007.

Twain, Mark. https://warprayer.org/.

Vance, Laurence M. *Erasmus on Christianity, War, and Soldiers*. Orlando: Vance Publications, 2020.

Weikart, Richard. "Scripture and Myth in Dietrich Bonhoeffer." *Fides et Historia* 25,1 (1993): 12—25.

Vance, Laurence M. "Joseph Judson Taylor, Man of Peace." https://libertarian christians.com/ 2015/03/18/man-of-peace/.

Williams, Tennessee. "Something by Tolstoy." https://bible.org/illustration/forgotten-love.

York, Alvin. *Sergeant York: His Own Life Story and War Diary*. New York: Doubleday Doran, 1928.

Index

INDEX

www.ingramcontent.com/pod-product-compliance
Lightning Source LLC
Chambersburg PA
CBHW071813090426
42737CB00012B/2073